Lottie Dod at the age of twenty.

Lottie Dod

Champion

of

Champions

The Story of an Athlete

by

Jeffrey Pearson

The costs of producing this book were met by members of the Dod and Worssam families in partnership with Countyvise Limited.

First published 1988 by Countyvise Limited, 1 & 3 Grove Road, Rock Ferry, Birkenhead, Wirral, Merseyside L42 3XS.

Copyright © Jeffrey Pearson, 1988.
Photoset and printed by Birkenhead Press Limited, 1 & 3 Grove Road, Rock Ferry, Birkenhead, Merseyside L42 3XS.

ISBN 0 907768 26 1.

*I dedicate this book to my daughters
Alicia and Victoria*

Acknowledgements

I should like to express my thanks to the following people, without whose help this study could not have been written:

Miss G. Anderson, Secretary, Ladies' Golf Union, Lt. Col. H. Boehm, President, The Royal Toxophilite Society, Mrs. M. Bray of the Grand National Archery Society, J.R. Davidson, Secretary of The Royal Liverpool Golf Club, Anthony Dod, Miss Barbara Dod, Mrs. Jane Dod, Michael Dod, Paul Dod, Philip Dod, John Graham of The Royal Liverpool Golf Club, Mrs. A. Wendy Hodkinson, Hon. Keeper, Simon Archery Collection, Mrs. P.E. Johnson, Librarian, Alpine Club, W.J. Kinsman, President of the London Archers, F.H. Lake, Archery Historian, Mrs. Anita Manning, Hon. Secretary, Irish Ladies' Hockey Union, Miss Maureen Miller, Chairman, Women Golfers' Museum, Miss Teresa Morris, Secretary, All England Women's Hockey Association, Miss P.F. Ward, Editor "Hockey Field", Miss Valerie Warren, Deputy Curator, Wimbledon Lawn Tennis Museum, Geoffrey Worssam and Ray Worssam.

List of Illustrations

Introduction

It is difficult to understand how Lottie Dod's name could ever havé faded into obscurity. Without doubt the greatest sportswoman of her time, and possibly of all time, she dazzled the British public with her achievements over the course of some twenty years. The first of the teenage tennis prodigies, when she won the Wimbledon Ladies Title in 1887 at the age of fifteen years and ten months she created a record that still stands. She then proceeded to prove that her victory had been no mere quirk of fate by winning the title on four more occasions. In fact, she was never beaten at Wimbledon. She was also a member of the winning partnership in several all-England doubles championships, and at various times she won all the other major United Kingdom tournaments. Turning from first-class tennis at the age of twenty-one, she became an international golfer, hockey player, and archer, and she achieved top honours in ice-skating. She was also proficient at riding and mountaineering. Particularly noteworthy among the honours she won in this post-tennis phase of her career were The British Ladies' Golf Championship in 1904, and the Silver Medal for Archery at the 1908 Olympic Games.

The press adored her. In Lottie Dod journalists thought they recognised the stuff of legends, and they set to work on it with enthusiasm. When she extended the reigning Wimbledon Champion, Maude Watson, to two advantage sets, at the age of thirteen, they established the eulogistic mood that they were to maintain over the following years by dubbing her "The Little Wonder". They acclaimed her victories with jubilation, vied with each other to find excuses for her defeats, and reported her comments on sport with the deference due to the pronouncements of an oracle. In 1888, when the *Pittsburgh Dispatch* dared to compare Lottie's style unfavourably with that of the American Champion, Mabel Cahill, and speculated on the result of any match between them, the sports correspondent of *The Star* commented testily, ". . . Miss Dod would in all probability give Miss Cahill half-30 and a beating."

Unfortunately, the matter was never tested on a tennis court.

It was a devotion that was to persist almost to the end of her long life. When all the surviving past Wimbledon Champions gathered foi a special Golden Jubilee celebration on the opening day of the 1926 Tournament, for example, the *Daily Telegraph* commented, "By far the most interesting of the women ex-champions was Miss Dod. In her day she was one of the finest of athletes and, although she first won the singles championship as long ago as 1887, she looked as if she could still give a good account of herself on the courts."

Writing in 1931, the Editor of *Country Life* remarked of Lottie, "Her name still sounds stirring in the ears of those who went to the old Wimbledon."

It was a type of adulation that seems to have been accorded to only one other person, Amy Johnson, a similarity that obviously inspired Wimbledon referee F.R. Burrows to write in the *Daily Sketch* of 22nd June, 1936, ". . . if flying had been invented in her time I have little doubt that Lottie Dod would have been the first girl to fly round the World."

As late as 1957 — just three years before her death — *World Sports* magazine still considered her to be interesting enough to justify the expense of sending a photographer from London to Milford-on-Sea, where she was then living.

That an athlete of such standing could be forgotten in a few short years would seem to be almost impossible. Yet such is the case. When Lottie died the flame of public interest, which had been lovingly tended by the Press for three-quarters of a century died with her. Enquiries published in national and regional magazines during the early "1980's" brought me just four replies.

The only possible explanation for this obscurity lies in the peculiarity of popular memory. The fact that "W.G. Grace" and "Suzanne Lenglen" are household names is due more to those great athletes' flamboyance than to their achievements. It is the Doctor's spade beard and irascible manner, and Lenglen's daring skirts and bandeaux, that are lodged in the public mind.

Lottie Dod was never flamboyant. A player of carefully-cultivated skills, split-second reactions, and relentless determination, her manner in the arena was invariably businesslike. While these qualities delighted the crowds who saw her in action, they did not produce the sort of simple visual impressions that could easily be passed from generation to generation. It is true that she was to become regarded as the model of tennis fashion, with her loose terra-cotta long-sleeved blouse with close-fitting embroidered collar and cuffs surmounting a dark blue skirt, but the tone she established was always one of quiet good taste.

Although I have been able to include many details that will help to reveal something of Lottie's character, this book is essentially an account of her sporting career rather than a biography. Lottie was a private person who gave few press interviews, and when she did — to borrow an idiom from one of the few sports she never tried — she kept her guard well up. That she possessed the super-ego which seems to be the necessary pre-requisite of champions is certain, but she knew how to control it when speaking to journalists, and in public her conduct and comments were invariably beyond reproach. Unfortunately, few of the letters and other private papers which might have helped me to acquire the sort of reasonably sound insight into her character that would be needed to write a full biographical study have survived, and to attempt to do so on the basis of fragmentary evidence would have been unjust to my subject.

For this book my principal sources have been the memories of Lottie's nephews and nieces, her scrapbooks, her photograph albums, and the contemporary press account of the events in which she competed, and of the interviews she gave. Whenever possible, I have supplied the dates and sources for the press accounts I have quoted, but many were copied from cuttings in Lottie's scrapbook and she occasionally failed to include all the relevant details.

This book is written in the conviction that the athletes whose memories we should celebrate are those who have adorned the sports they have played with their skills, their sportsmanship, and their selfless contributions to the betterment of those sports. On that basis there has never been one more fitting to be numbered with the immortals than Lottie Dod.

Chapter One

Charlotte Dod was born on 21st September, 1871 at Bebington, Cheshire, the fourth child of Joseph Dod, a wealthy Liverpool cotton broker and banker, and his wife, Margaret.

To-day a place of prosperous suburban sprawl, in Lottie's time Bebington was a peaceful village, standing in surroundings that, as late as 1912, were described by one M. O'Mahoney in the following terms:

"Spreading sycamores, graceful ash trees, and stunted oaks throng in on either side, while rising to meet them is every conceivable manner of briar and bramble known to Cheshire wilderness. Convolvulus that was delicately green, and is now purple in fading beauty, twines amidst the sloe bushes. Briony runs wreathing to and fro through the tangled hedges. Under the gnarled boughs are glimpses of half-hidden pools, and the odour of gorse and bracken goes with you all the way."

When Charlotte was two the family moved from the modest house where she had been born to "Edgeworth", a large "Queen Anne" style gabled house, which Joseph had built in spacious wooded grounds on the outskirts of the village. The house was named in accordance with the Dod family tradition of calling their houses "Edge" — this or "Edge-that", to honour the memory of Sir Antony Dod of Edge, who had commanded the English archers at Agincourt, and from whom the Family claim descent.

Family Group at "Edgeworth" about 1890.
Left to right:
Fanny Apinall (Cousin), Willy, Lottie, Margaret Dod and Tony.

From the little that is now known about Joseph he appears to have been an interesting man. After inheriting some £5,000 from his father when he was twenty-seven, he invested it to such good effect that he was able to retire at the age of thirty-nine. When he died, ten years later, he left Margaret wealthy enough to maintain "Edgeworth", together with its domestic staff, and to support herself and her children in considerable comfort until she died in 1901, and then to leave the children enough money to free them from the need to work for the remainder of their lives, had they so chosen. In the event Lottie's sister, Ann, married into a prosperous London family and spent much of her time attending to her domestic duties, and one brother, Anthony, chose to engage in what may, perhaps, be best described as small-scale farming. William and Lottie, both of whom remained single, never worked for their living in the course of their long lives.

Which is not the same as stating that they never did any useful work. Far from it. All four Dod children became first rate athletes, and, unpaid, provided the sort of entertainment that is now provided by professionals. In addition, they helped to raise large sums for various worthwhile causes by playing in charity matches. Nor was enjoyment of their skills confined to the wealthier classes: in 1904, when word spread through the Clydeside shipyards that the great Lottie Dod was playing in the final of the British Ladies' Golf Championship at Troon, hundreds of workers took an unofficial day's holiday to see the match.

Joseph was an expert photographer. In the days when photography was still very much in its infancy he produced prints that many modern enthusiasts might envy. A considerable number still exist, and it would be difficult to find one that is not both clear and well-balanced. As might be expected, his subjects were his family, his home, his employees — the housekeeper, the maids, and the gardener — his fellow members of Bebington Bowling Club, and various scenes about the village.

Somewhat surprisingly for a man of substance, he served for a time in the local unit of the Royal Engineer Volunteer Force (the equivalent of the modern Territorial Army) with the lowly rank of sapper.

Even less is known about Margaret than about Joseph. One or two photogrphs survive, which portray her as a rather severe-looking woman, but, then, Victorian matrons did tend to look severe in posed photographs.

On the census forms for 1871 and '81 she described her occupation as 'housekeeper', but whether this reveals a sense of humour, or was an attempt to mislead prying officialdom is a matter for speculation.

What is certain is that she could, and did, employ a housekeeper herself, and that she loved good furniture. When one of her last housekeepers, Ada Stott, married in 1895 Margaret Dod presented her with a very fine walnut worktable. Two months later, evidently regretting the impulse which had made her part with the piece, she offered to buy it back for forty pounds. It was a handsome offer. Forty pounds in 1895 must have represented something like a year's wages for Ada, but she stoutly refused to accept it.

Perhaps Margaret found some consolation for the loss of the worktable, when in the following year, she was able to snap up eight Regency chairs for a pound each.

Ann was the eldest of the children, being eight when Charlotte was born; William was four years older than Charlotte; and Anthony was just a year older. At home they were known as : "Annie", "Willy" "Tony" and "Lottie". Among the family and their close friends Tony was also known as "Bones", a nickname that was suggested by his slight build and one that accompanied him throughout his life.

Charlotte seems to have used both names — "Charlotte" and "Lottie" according to a fairly consistent formula. On formal occasions and for signing official letters and documents she used her proper name; at home, among friends, and for anything to do with sport, it was "Lottie", even to the extent of having "Lottie Dod" engraved on her trophies.

The children were educated at home by a series of tutors, a common arrangements among upper-middle class families at the time. Quite possibly it was these tutors who fired their enthusiasm for the wide range of artistic skills they were all to exhibit. Annie, for example, was a gifted artist in both oils and water colours. Lottie was the musician of the family, playing the piano, the banjo, and something called "the American organ". She also sang in a rich contralto voice, and she was a member of a local choir. Both Willy and Tony were interested in woodworking and woodcarving, and photography.

The Dod children shared a passion for games and sports of all kind. Golf, archery, skating, bowls, croquet, bridge and chess were almost a way of life for them, and they were all to become champions at something or other.

Among her many other accomplishments, Annie was a fine tennis player and golfer; she skated well, and was awarded the much-coveted three-star (i.e. first class) badge of the National Skating Association; and, in her later years, she was the subject of an article in a glossy magazine, which maintained that she was probably the best woman billiards player in England.

Willy was to win the gold medal for archery at the 1908 Olympics, and the National Archery Championship of the United Kingdom - twice. He was also a first-class golfer, winning the South of Ireland

Championship in 1901, by defeating S.H. Fry, who was to be runner-up at the British Championship the following year.

A good shot, Willy tried the then respectable activity of big-game hunting at least once.

In February, 1898 he sailed from Liverpool to New York, en route to Canada to shoot bears. One of his fellow passengers on the ship was Rudyard Kipling. They met and, in one way or another, the conversation turned to the somewhat unusual spelling of Willy's surname with its single 'd' ending. "I suppose what is good enough for God is good enough for Dod," remarked Kipling.

When he returned to England at the end of his expedition Willy was able to present the Grenadier Guards with two bearskins.

In his early teens Tony suffered from severe asthma, and, to pass the long days when he was confined to bed, he studied chess. He became so proficient that on one occasion he played blindfolded against thirteen, non-blindfolded, local chess enthusiasts simultaneously, and beat most of them. In 1902 he won the Chess Championships of both Cheshire and Lancashire.

Many years later, when his son, Philip, was at school in Devonshire he heard that one of the masters was a chess player and, knowing that Tony was always keen to play new opponents, he suggested to the teacher that they might play a game or two.

"Well no, Philip, I don't think it would be quite fair. You see, I'm the West of England Champion," was the answer.

Philip hastened to assure him that his father would be willing to take his chances. The meeting was arranged and Tony proceeded to sweep the West of England Champion off the board three times in one evening.

Like their father, both Willy and Tony were keen photographers and many of the photographs in this book were taken by one or other of them.

When Lottie was nine the Family was struck by the lawn tennis mania that was then sweeping through the leisured classes.

Invented as recently as 1873, the game was so new that no-one at "Edgeworth" had actually seen a tennis court. When two courts — one grass and the other hard — were laid out there, the stop-netting was at first erected very close to the base lines, because neither the contractors nor the Dods realised that a long run-back was needed.

It seems that, at first, Willy and Tony were afflicted by the traditional impatience of boys with their sisters, particularly when their friends called to play, and did their best to chase them off the courts. With her four years seniority, and much spirited support from Lottie, Annie was able to assert the girls' right to play whenever they wished to do so.

Lottie Dod aged nine.

Chapter Two

It was at the age of eleven that Lottie made her tournament debut. In partnership with Annie she entered the Ladies' Doubles event at the Northern Championship, which in 1883 was held at Manchester.

Following a bye in the first round, they were beaten in the second round, 6-5, 6-1, by a local pair, but they went on to win first prize in the Consolation Doubles.

One particularly perceptive sports writer commented, "Miss L. Dod should be heard of in the future, as though only an eleven year old, she showed really good form, and not only served well, but displayed tactics worthy of much older players. She played from the back of the court with both skill and judgement."

In 1884 Lottie entered two tournaments, the first at Waterloo and the other at the Northern Championships, which were held that year at Liverpool. She played in the Ladies' Doubles at both tournaments partnered by Annie, and in the Mixed Doubles at Waterloo partnered by Tony. She and Tony were beaten in the first round, but the girls reached the finals of both Ladies' events before being defeated.

1885 was the first of Lottie's great years. It was the year in which she served notice — both literally and metaphorically — that she was to become a challenger for the highest honours in the game.

She entered the same tournaments that she had entered in the previous year, playing in the singles as well as the doubles.

At Waterloo she was completely triumphant, winning the singles title by beating Margaret Bracewell, a very experienced player, the Ladies' Doubles in partnership with Annie, and the Mixed Doubles with a new partner, John Edmonson.

It was, however, at the Northern Championships that she caused the tennis sensation of the year by winning through to meet, and almost beat, the reigning Wimbledon Champion, Maude Watson, in the final. For Miss Watson, a player who had dominated the ladies' game for over three years, the experience of meeting a thirteen-year-old child who volleyed and smashed with a power that no woman had previously commanded must have been traumatic.

The final was a close fought contest, but Maude was at the height of her powers, a seasoned campaigner, and a shrewd judge of her opponents' play, while Lottie was still learning. Detecting a weakness in Lottie's backhand, Miss Watson pressed hard on that wing to secure the match, but not before Lottie had extended her to two advantage sets 8-6, 7-5.

1883 Lottie and Annie. Photograph taken to mark their first appearance in an Open Tournament (The Northern).

While Lottie may have been disappointed at her failure to beat Maude Watson, the Dod girls had good reason for jubilation when they defeatd the Wimbledon Champion and her sister, Lilian, in the second round of the Ladies' Doubles, before pressing on to win the event by vanquishing two other top players, Margaret Bracewell and Bea Langrishe, in the final.

So enthusiastic were the Press about Lottie's performance that they dubbed her, "The Little Wonder".

It was a title that was destined to last for a couple of years only, not because Lottie ceased to be any less wonderful, but because she grew to the point where she was no longer 'little'. As an adult she was, in fact, rather above average height. When she was eighteen the *Daily Chronicle* described her in the following terms: ". . . she is as well developed as most women of five and twenty. Miss Dod is a little above the medium height,* her head well set on a pair of solid shoulders, good muscular biceps and an admirable figure. Her jet black hair and eyes and oval face give her the appearance of a "Southern girl", to borrow an expression from the States."

It is a description that may also convey something of Annie's appearance, because tbere was said to have been a marked resemblance between the sisters.

Almost certainly, Lottie's outfit on court during her early years in the public eye helped to promote an impression of diminutive size. As a junior she was allowed to wear short skirts, instead of the voluminous garments worn by women, until she was sixteen.

Annie, too, had.developed into a first-class player. One of the first women to wield an effective overarm service, her repertoire of strokes included a particularly wicked drop shot. In this same year of 1885 Annie won the Scottish Open Championship at Moffat, and then proceeded to retain it in the two following years. Lottie, who did not travel to Scotland when Annie first won the title, refused to enter the event while Annie was still Champion, presumably regarding that particular title as her sister's preserve.

In the years that followed the partnership between the Dod sisters proved to be a powerful one. Indeed, they became widely acknowledged to be the leading women's doubles pair in the country. A feature of their play, which was regarded as startingly novel at the time but is now accepted as normal, was the tactic of both advancing to the net as soon as possible after the ball was in play, to dominate their opponents' court.

Among their many achievements, they retained the Northern title until 1889, and they won the West of England title three times.

---

*She was, in fact, 5' 6 1/2" tall – J.P.

Lottie Dod aged 14 – "The Little Wonder".

The boys then tried to discourage the girls by refusing to modify the ferocity of their strokes in deference to their femininity.

To that Annie and Lottie responded by practising hard, driving and volleying against a garden wall until they could play well enough to hold their own when they were on court with the boys. Playing against girls of their own age they became almost invincible.

Occasional tennis parties soon became a feature of life at "Edgeworth". Usually held on a Wednesday or a Saturday, they began at about 3.00 p.m. with a men's doubles. At 4.30 p.m., or thereabouts, Margaret presided over a monumental tea set out on her terrace, refilling cups and keeping the maids scurrying round the tables with heaped plates of sandwiches, scones and cakes. Everyone drank vast amounts of tea, and the talk was of nothing but tennis tactics and forthcoming tournaments. After tea, play continued until the shadows lengthened across the courts, when those who had some distance to travel took to their bicycles or pony traps.

Despite the social aspect of these parties they were very different from the pat-ball gatherings that were held at so many later Victorian houses. At "Edgeworth" tennis was regarded as a serious business. Many of the guests were county players, and matches were played at a furious pace with no quarter asked or given. Among the distinguished players who became frequent visitors to the house was future Wimbledon Champion Joshua Pim — known as "the ghost", he was apparently even thinner than Tony — and the identical twin brothers Wilfred and Herbert Baddeley, who were to win the All-England Doubles Championship twice. When Lottie was at the height of her powers, three times Wimbledon singles Champion Wilfred observed that she was, ". . . fifteen better than any other woman player."

Believing that over-indulgence in any one sport can lead to boredom and poor performance, the Dods varied their activities by playing croquet, golf, bowls, and the many other pastimes that were available to them.

So addicted were they to sport that they followed these pastimes seven days a week, a practice that caused a rift in the wider Dod family when James Dod, a distant cousin and a christian of the Old School, complained, in vain, to Margaret about their violation of the Sabbath.

With the exception of Tony, the Bebington Dods were, indeed, largely indifferent to religion. Tony regularly attended church throughout his life, but he reserved the right to play tennis, or any other game, afterwards.

Such, then, was the furnace in which Lottie's tennis skills were forged. After just two seasons she was playing so well that she was accepted as a member of Rock Ferry Tennis Club, Birkenhead, at the age of eleven — five years younger than the official minimum age.

Edgeworth in the "1880s". Lottie, Willy, Tony and an unknown friend seated by the tennis courts.

Unhappily, Fate was to prevent their playing as a pair in the All England Ladies' Doubles Tournament.

Lottie began the 1886 season by causing an even greater sensation than the one she had produced at the 1885 Northern Championships: she beat Maude Watson in the final of the West of England Championships at Bath. For tennis devotees who had not seen her in action the result must have been almost unbelievable. Maude Watson had not been beaten in open singles since she started playing first-class tennis in 1881, and Lottie's triumph had brought an end to a run of fifty-five victories, in the course of which Maude had dropped only twelve sets.

It is certainly true that she had been unfortunate in the draw. While Lottie had faced opposition that had been no more than competent in the early rounds, Maude had been extended by some of the best players of the day: Margaret Bracewell; Grace Gibbs, the holder; Blanche Bingley, who was to wrest the Wimbledon crown from her later that year; and Louise Martin, who was to become Irish Champion no fewer than nine times.

Even so, there seems little doubt that Lottie played brilliantly in the final. Moving coolly and confidently about the court, she drove and volleyed like a girl inspired, returning her opponent's severest services with ease, and punishing all attempts to break down her backhand. So violent was Lottie's volleying that the kerchief she wore as a coif to keep her hair in place fluttered off into the crowd on a number of occasions. Thereafter she wore the peaked cap that was to become part of her image in the public mind.

In those far-off days the prizes awarded at tournaments appear to have varied widely both in nature and value, and purely commemorative cups and plaques were less commonly awarded than they are now. While money prizes were, of course, unthinkable, there can be little doubt that many modern professionals would have settled for the handsome diamond pendant that Lottie received for winning at Bath.

She won a second title at the meeting in partnership with Annie.

The remainder of the year was something of an anti-climax for Lottie. It became obvious that she could still learn something from the more experienced players, and she won no more singles titles that season. At Cheltenham she was beaten by Blanch Bingley; at the Northern Championships Maude Watson gained her revenge by beating her in the final 7-5, 6-3, and at the Derbyshire Championship she was vanquished by May Langrishe.

There was, however, some satisfaction for her in doubles victories at the Northern Tournament in partnership with Annie, and in The All England Doubles at Buxton in partnership with May Langrishe — Annie being temporarily incapacitated by a chill.

That chill proved to be a fateful one for Annie. It not only deprived her of the opportunity to partner Lottie in the All England Ladies' Doubles Event of 1886, but in those of the following two years also. Having won the Championship with May Langrishe, Lottie was obliged to continue defending it with her, and, by the time she was free to partner her sister in the event, Annie was living in London.

During the Derbyshire Meeting at Buxton a novel cricket match was played between a team of women and a team of men competitors, the men batting left-handed and with broomsticks. To the delight of the 2,000 spectators who were drawn to the event, the ladies won with two minutes to spare. Lottie, who was required to bat in only one innings, scored 14 and bowled to such good effect that she produced a "hat-trick".

1887 was the year in which Lottie secured her place among the tennis immortals. Her apprenticeship was over, and from the first tournament of the season at Dublin she was to play with a power that never faltered throughout the remainder of her tennis career.

At Dublin she won the singles, beating Maude Watson 6-4, 6-3, in the championship round, and the Mixed Doubles title in partnership with Ernest Renshaw. It is, perhaps, a comment on her play that the great Ernest Renshaw, then at the height of his powers, and holding the sixth of his seven Wimbledon singles titles, should have considered a fifteen-year old girl to be a worthwhile partner in an open event.

A week later at Bath, Lottie swept through the singles rounds without losing a set before she again defeated Maude Watson in the final 7-5, 6-4. She also retained the Ladies' Doubles title with Annie, and won the Mixed Doubles with the American James Dwight.

Her performance at the Northern Championships was even more convincing. In the singles event she beat the brilliant Irish player Louise Martin 6-0, 6-2; May Langrishe 6-1, 6-2; Margaret Bracewell 6-2, 6-2; and, in the final, Maude Watson 6-2, 6-1. That is, she won the title by beating some of the best players of the day without losing more than two games in any set.

In the Doubles event she and Annie won the title for the third consecutive year.

These successes encouraged Lottie to enter the Wimbledon Tournament, which was held in those days at Worple Road, Wimbledon. She was then fifteen years and ten months old.   It has been claimed that the task she faced was a relatively easy one: at a time when an entry of twenty for the Wimbledon Ladies' Championship was regarded as a large one, there were just six competitors in the 1887 event, and both Maude Watson and Louise Martin were absent.

Even so, and despite Lottie's widely-acclaimed successes, many spectators were inclined to regard her entry as something of a joke. After all, the defending champion, Blanche Bingley, was a formidable competitor, of whom Frank Burrow wrote, "She owed as much of her success to her unconquerable resolution as to her actual strokes, though her powers of running also had a good deal to do with it. She never volleyed unless forced but her powerful forehand driving, the stroke made at the top of the bound and a little top spin applied, was too much for most of her opponents. Her backhand was purely defensive . . . . unlike the generality of early women players, she served overhand, but it was not a service of any great terrors. One thing that differentiated her from nearly every woman player in the game's history, was that she invariably wore white gloves."

In the event, Lottie, who drew a bye in the first round, easily vanquished her opponents in the second and third rounds, and then proceeded to beat Miss Bingley 6-2, 6-0 in the Challenge Round.

At Wimbledon, and at many other tournaments, the system at that time was that champions were not required to play through all the rounds, but stood out to wait for a challenger to emerge from the other competitors. The title was then decided in a championship round between the holder and the challenger.

So completely did Lottie control the play in the championship round that after two-all was called in the first set she reeled off the next ten games to clinch the match. The second set lasted for a mere ten minutes, during which time the crowd cheered every point she won with cries of "Lottie! Lottie!".

There can be no doubt that the circumstances which favoured Lottie had absolutely no effect on the result. She would have won the title if all the best women players in the World had been playing.

The fact was she was playing a new sort of tennis. It has been said of Lottie Dod that she played the all-court game ahead of her time, the chief characteristics of her style being an uncanny anticipation of her opponents' play that enabled her to be in the right place at the right moment, and a mastery of the full range of strokes.

It was Lottie who introduced the volley into women's tennis, using a mighty round-arm stroke whenever she could take the ball above net height. Holding her racquet with the knuckles of her fingers facing the net (technically the western grip), she hit the ball very hard and with a slight underspin that made it skid off the grass in a way that caused her opponents great problems. She changed her grip when making backhand drives, a technique that is standard today but was, at that time, highly unorthodox. The one grip, now known as the continental grip, was almost standard then.

Years later A. Wallis Myers wrote of her play: "In the matter of technique she was absolutely without a weak point; her forehand drive had the pace of a man's — it was made quietly and very decidedly and with absolute freedom and its power and length took one by surprise; she volleyed with great judgement and accuracy; she had a powerful smash, and this though she served underhand." *(Fifty Years of Wimbledon - 1926).*

Lottie deliberately stuck to the underarm delivery because she believed that the overarm service was a waste of energy that brought no compensating advantages. In her contributory article to the *Badminton Library of Sports* she wrote: "I do think ladies' overhand service a great waste of strength."

Lottie did not play in any other open singles events in 1887. At Taunton she played handicap singles — handicap events being common at the time — and won the prize despite owing the other competitors thirty in every game, and then went on to complete her year's triumphs at Buxton by retaining the All England Doubles title with May Langrishe and winning the Mixed with James Dwight.

Such was Lottie's reputation at the beginning of the 1888 season that the Committee of the West of England Tournament took the remarkable decision to impose a handicap of 15 on her in what was advertised as an open singles event.

It was a favour which Blanche Bingley, with her name now changed by marriage to Blanche Hillyard, scorned when she met Lottie in the opening round, and which she proceeded to prove that she did not need. Ever the fighter, Mrs. Hillyard took the first set 10-8, before Lottie raised the standard of her play to win the next two sets 6-3, 6-0. She then went on to win the title, despite the handicap.

Another closely fought encounter took place when Blanche Hillyard qualified to meet Lottie, the holder, in the challenge round at the Northern Championships, before Lottie emerged as the victor, 6-3, 9-7.

In the championship round at Wimbledon she again faced Blanche Hillyard and, urged on by the now familiar cries of "Lottie" from the record crowd, defeated her 6-3, 6-3 in just 35 minutes.

During 1888 Lottie also played in a number of successful doubles partnerships. With Annie she won the West of England Ladies' Title for the third consecutive year, and the Scarborough Title. At Buxton she renewed her partnership with May Langrishe to win the All England Ladies' Doubles Championship for the third year running, and she won the Derbyshire Mixed Doubles Title in partnership with Drummond Hamilton. At Exmouth Lawn Tennis Club, picturesquely situated at the foot of Beacon Hill facing the estuary of the River Exe, she partnered Ernest Renshaw to defeat Mrs. Hillyard and her husband G.W. Hillyard 6-1, 4-6, 6-4, in the Mixed Doubles Final.

Exmouth 1888. Lottie with Ernest Renshaw, seven times winner of the Wimbledon Men's title.

Towards the end of the season Lottie played in several interesting exhibition matches, against men. At Exmouth her opponent was Ernest Renshaw. During the course of a spirited encounter between the two Wimbledon Champions, in which Renshaw owed 30, Lottie won the first set before Renshaw took the next two sets for the match, with the final score standing at 2-6, 7-5, 7-5. At Scarborough she was more successful, beating Harry Grove who owed half-30, 1-6, 6-0, 6-3, and William Renshaw owing 30, 6-2, 6-4.

Another interesting feature of the season was the emergence of what might now be considered to be something akin to a Lottie Dod Fan Club. It became the fashion for parties of society girls to visit nearby tournaments when Lottie was playing in them, and some even followed her about the country to study her play and acclaim her victories. At Wimbledon, when one girl asked her the secret of her success, Lottie replied, "Well, I never lose my head in a game, and experience has taught never to lose my temper. I think tennis a capital game to teach a girl self-control."

Imagine, then, the extent of the general disappointment when she failed to defend her Wimbledon title in 1889. The more so because she had played with her customary brilliance in the early part of the season. Her absence gave rise to much speculation and when her explanation for it became public knowledge, several months later, it can hardly have pleased those tennis enthusiasts who had been disappointed. It seems that in the weeks immediately before the

c1890 Lottie and Tony on court at "Edgeworth".

Tournament Lottie and Annie were sailing with friends off the Western Coast of Scotland, and Lottie was enjoying herself so much that she decided to stay there instead of returning to England to defend her title.

The only open singles event in which Lottie played that year was at the Northern Tournament, where she successfully defended her title for the third successive year, beating Blanche Hillyard 6-8, 6-3, 6-3.

There was, however, a disappointment for Lottie and Annie when they lost the Northern Ladies Doubles title to Bertha and Mary Steadman in the Challenge Round, after having held it for the four previous years. It was almost the end of their partnership. Only once more did the Dod sisters play together — in a handicap event at Newcastle-on-Tyne — before Annie married Ernest Taylor Worssam, a brewer with Whitbreads, and went to live with him in London.

In the following year, 1890, Lottie again baffled tennis devotees, this time by a complete absence from the tennis circuit. There appears to be no explanation for her behaviour other than that of boredom with the game. Certainly there was nothing wrong with her. She played golf, croquet, and even tennis enough at club level, but no competition tennis.

In 1891 she competed in just one tournament, Wimbledon, where she regained the title by defeating Blanche Hillyard 6-2, 6-1.

This, almost complete, rest from competition tennis appears to have revived some of her interest in the game, and in 1892 she made a return to the tournament circuit at Dublin.

There she was sensationally beaten in the second round of the Open Singles Event by the brilliant Louise Martin, who was aided by that special luck which is said to smile on the Irish. After Miss Martin had captured the first set with some fine serving and volleying, Lottie fought back to win the second, and, with her opponent visibly tiring, was leading 2-1 in the third when a heavy shower caused play to be suspended for twenty minutes. When play was resumed the rested Miss Martin recovered her best form to win the match 6-2, 2-6, 7-5. It was the first defeat that Lottie had suffered in open singles since 1886.

Three weeks later Lottie played Louise Martin again, in the final — that is, the round that decided who was to go on to challenge the holder — of the Open Singles Event at the Northern Championships, which were held that year at Liverpool.

It seems that the dose of defeat had been exactly the right tonic to restore all of Lottie's zest for tennis. She brushed aside her first three opponents with the loss of just six games, as if she were impatient to come to grips with Miss Martin, who had been assigned to the other half of the draw in the expectation that they would both win through to meet in the final, an expectation that they proceeded to fulfil.

Lottie Dod aged twenty.

Record crowds thronged to see the match, but the closely-fought encounter they were obviously hoping to see did not materialise. Instead, Lottie treated them to a display that looked more like an exhibition than a match.

After losing the first game, she won the next twelve with a barnstorming series of brilliantly executed drives, volleys, and smashes, that left her opponent helpless and the crowd breathless. Even her normally vociferous suporters fell silent as events on court rolled onwards with the awesome inevitability of a public execution. It took Lottie just thirty minutes to shatter any illusions that Louise Martin — or anyone else — might have harboured that she was losing her touch.

Certainly, the champion, Miss Stannel, was impressed. She needed no time for reflection before deciding not to defend her title, and Lottie was awarded the prize by her default.

At the same tournament she won the Ladies' Doubles with a new partner, Helen Jackson, and the All England Mixed Doubles title with Tony.

The Mixed Doubles triumph must have been particularly satisfying for Tony. Although over the years he had often partnered Lottie in open tournaments and reached the finals on many occasions, this, the most important, was the first one that they had

Liverpool 1892 Northern Championships. Lottie (in cap) and Helen Jackson play Mrs. W.H. Pickering and Miss Pickthall, 6-1, 6-3.

won together. The fact was that while both Willy and Tony were good players, they had not achieved the same standing in men's tennis as that attained by their sisters in the women's game.

Also at the 1892 Northern Meeting Lottie played in another of those rather curious novelty matches of which the Victorians seemed to have been so fond. Partnered by Herbert Baddeley, she played and vanquished Ernest Renshaw and George Hillyard. Translated into modern terms that is much the same as Steffi Graf sharing with, say, Ivan Lendl in the defeat of Stefan Edberg and Boris Becker.

At Wimbledon Lottie maintained her form to crush yet another challenge from Blanche Hillyard 6-1, 6-1.

The Press was ecstatic. "Miss Dod has again with comparative ease won the Championship at Wimbledon," reported *The Lady's Pictorial* which continued, "and all who saw her fine play and complete mastery of the situation in her different contests must allow that she is very far superior to all her sister exponents of the game, and quite worthy of the position she holds."

The Field asked, "What is the secret of Miss Dod's extraordinary success?" and then attempted to answer its own question. "It is, of course, very difficult to say; but we can readily affirm that it is due as much to correct judgement, to steady perseverance, as to physical superiority. Indeed, Miss Dod is by no means extraordinarily gifted

Edgeworth 1892. Lottie and Tony (All England Mixed Doubles Champions) play the Baddeley Brothers (All England Mens' Doubles Champions).

with muscular strength, she is not particularly tall; but she is wonderfully active, and she recognises the great necessity for complete freedom of action while playing, and very sensibly adopts a costume which gives free play to her limbs. But above all, in lawn tennis, as in most other games, moral forces come into play; a tennis genius is undoubtedly one who has an infinite capacity for taking pains. There are brilliant erratic spirits in the lawn tennis, as well as in other worlds, who may dazzle the untutored beholder by their extraordinary dash and vigour; but let the fortune of the game go against them for a while, and they lose heart, commit most deplorable blunders and seem to lose the capacity for playing at all. Miss Dod is not one of these; brilliant she undoubtedly is; but hers is no fitful brilliancy — it is rather a steady glow, which seems to grow brighter and more intense as victory succeeds victory, and triumph follows triumph".

In 1893 — the last year in which Lottie played in first-class tennis — she competed in just two tournaments: The Northern, staged at Manchester, and Wimbledon.

At both Manchester and Wimbledon she again defeated her most persistent rival, Blanche Hillyard, in the challenge rounds, to retain the titles, but not without some difficulty. On both occasions the matches ran to three sets. At Manchester the score was 6-2, 3-6, 7-5, and at Wimbledon it was 6-8, 6-1, 6-4. During the third set at Wimbledon Lottie fell heavily and many of the sports columnists who were watching later wrote that they had thought she would be obliged to retire, but, after a short rest, she was able to continue.

So ended Lottie Dod's tennis career.

Although she was only twenty-one it was a career that had spanned eleven seasons, during which she had been defeated a mere five times in open singles — twice by Maude Watson and once each by Blanche Hillyard, May Langrishe and Louise Martin. Of these defeats one only had been sustained after she had reached her fifteenth birthday.

Her decision to retire from competition tennis was based largely on boredom. There was a complete absence of challengers who might have offered her an interesting game, and she seemed to have grown weary of winning. Years later she told Ray Worssam — Annie's son — that she had abandoned tournament tennis because she did not want to be thought "a pot hunter" and because she wanted to see how well she could do at other sports.

In 1899 Lottie gave one of the very few press interviews she ever gave, to a journalist from *The Lady's Pictorial*, in which she talked about her tennis career. " 'I have been particularly fond of outdoor pastimes all my life,' she said. 'In fact, I love an outdoor life above all others, and every open-air exercise appeals to me, but beyond all the rest I love lawn tennis. I began to play when I was nine years old on this grass court in the garden (i.e. at "Edgeworth"), and on which I have performed every summer since. I played mostly with my brother, Mr. Anthony Dod, and perhaps it is because I have mostly played with men that I have learnt to play such a 'strong' game. At least,' she laughed, 'I believe I am supposed to play a strong game. Of course, if you play constantly against strong players, you naturally learn to play a harder game and then the average man's stroke is undoubtedly much more powerful and swift than even the most expert woman player's.

'You always play a volleying game, do you not?'

'Well, not always. You see, it depends so much on the set you are playing, though it is my custom to follow up the ball, and take up a position three feet inside the service line. No, I never 'went into training' even for the championship. How did I come to go in for it? Well, it was like this : as a child I really played well, and had plenty of smaller successes, and everyone thought I should try the Championship. So I did, and won it from Miss Bingley in 1887. Then I won it again the next year. The third summer I was yachting in Scotland with friends, and we were having such a good time that, though I wanted to win it three years running very much, I could not make up my mind to leave the yacht, so I let it go that year altogether. In 1891 I thought I'd really like to win it properly three years in succession, so I went in for it again, and won consecutively in that year and in 1892 and 1893.'

It is very difficult indeed, to induce Miss Dod to talk about her numerous successes, and I was obliged to find out from other sources the stories of most of her triumphs. From 1886 to 1893 was one long line for her of brilliant successes, and she has won in all sixty-one prizes for lawn tennis alone; forty-one of these are first prizes, eleven are second prizes, one is a third prize and one a consolation prize besides seven championship momentos and challenge cups — in all a goodly list. In 1887 Miss Dod was actually the holder of five championships — 'The United Kingdom' in singles and ladies doubles; the 'Irish'; 'Northern'; and 'West of England'.

'Tell me about some of the most exciting matches or sets you have ever played,' I said.

'Truly, there is not much I can tell you,' she answered. 'I have played so much and in so many matches, and every set becomes exciting to me when it is played by good players, that it is difficult to particularise. However, one match I remember well as an exceptionally exciting and interesting one, was played on our own lawn here between the Brothers Baddeley and my brother * and

---

*Tony. It was, in fact, a match between the 1893 Men's and Mixed All England Doubles Champions.

35

myself. I scarcely remember the scoring, but they gave my brother and me half fifteen, which made us exactly even; and the play was very close as we were all in most excellent form.'

'How do you feel about playing in public?'

'Well, you know, I think that all real lovers of the game become so interested in the set they are playing that they almost forget that they are being watched. One concentrates oneself, so to speak, on ones own play, and on ones opponent's, and has no time to remember anything else at all.' " *(Lady's Pictorial. Unspecified date 1899).*

Chapter Three

In the decade that followed Lottie pursued an amazingly wide range of sports, both competitive and non-competitve. While golf was an interest second only to tennis, she also found time to try climbing, tobogganing, and hockey and to excel at many of them.

She also continued to play social tennis at home, at Rock Ferry and other tennis clubs, and elsewhere.

During this period a close friendship developed between the "Edgeworth" Dods and the Leghs of Lyme Hall, Cheshire. Piers F. Legh, his wife Blanche, and their daughters, Aice and Beata, were all archers of national standing. The Leghs became regular visitors to "Edgeworth" and there can be no doubt that Lottie and her brothers learned to draw a bow at Lyme.

In December 1895, Lottie, Tony and Miss Pennington Legh a niece of Piers Legh, joined a party of friends who travelled to St. Moritz for the winter, leaving Willy at home to keep his mother company.

With the exchange rate standing at 25 Swiss francs to the pound, British visitors could stay for long periods in Switzerland very cheaply, and it was the patronage of the wealthy Britons who flocked to places like St. Moritz and Davos during the late nineteenth century that established them as winter restorts.

Lottie, Tony, and Pennington Legh stayed at the now-famous Kulm Hotel, overlooking the Lake, but the actual hotel at which particular tourists stayed had little effect on their sport or socialising. Visitors mingled freely at each other's hotels, in the town, and on the ice and curling rinks. They spent their days skating, tobogganing, curling, climbing, playing a form of ice hockey, and even engaging in such improbable activities as cricket on the frozen surface of Lake Moritz. A few experimented with the infant sport of downhill ski-ing. During the evenings they found their entertainment at dances and fancy dress parties, and by presenting amateur theatricals and concerts, occasions when the musical talents of people like Lottie were much in demand. In short, St. Moritz was nothing less than the setting for a gigantic house party, at which aristocrats, socialites, distinguished athletes, and a host of lesser beings pursued amusement with relentless determination, while their activities were chronicled by *The Alpine Post*, a weekly English Language newspaper, which was dedicated to the purpose. Among those its columns recorded as visiting St. Moritz at the same time as Lottie and Company were The Duchess of Manchester, Lady Alice Montague, the Honourable Victoria Gibson, and the Vicomte de Monzilly.

Lottie had learned to skate at Liverpool Ice Rink in the now-outmoded "English Style", in which the hands were held to the sides or clasped behind the back. She had gained the "Three-Star" Badge — the highest award — of The National Skating Association, and one of her reasons for travelling to Switzerland was to attempt the St. Moritz Ladies' Skating Test, which was widely regarded as the most demanding and prestigious challenge offered to women by the Skating World. After a month's training, she passed the Test on 15th January, 1896.

Somewhat surprisingly, perhaps, she also played a considerable amount of tennis on the Kulm's hard court, for the most part to satisfy the demands of those who wanted to see the great Lottie Dod in action. Although the games in which she was involved were played in a spirit that was far from intense, they were reported by *The Alpine Post* with the solemnity due to a championship match.

"Lovers of Lawn Tennis have had the pleasure of witnessing some really first-class play on the Kulm Court during the past week. Miss Dod, the Lady Champion, and brother, owing to a generally expressed desire to see them play, kindly consented to do so, and on Sunday last opposed Miss Pennington Legh and Doctor Holland. The latter was decidedly off colour, but Miss Legh played as we have never seen her play before. Her volleying and back-hand strokes across the court were tremendously strong, and she scored repeatedly by them, even against the powerful combination on the other side of the net. Miss Dod, though palpably out of practice, gave constant evidence of the great strength of her game, and made some beautiful

1897 St. Moritz. Tennis at the Kulm. Lottie (back to camera) and Tony play Miss Pemmington Legh and Doctor Holland.

Mrs. Elizabeth Main at St. Moritz 1895.

strokes; she and her brother, who volleyed very correctly, proved too strong for the other pair, and won by two sets to love." (1st February, 1896).

The tennis court at the Kulm was always in demand, but when some of the guests suggested to the proprietor, a man named Badrutt, that a second court would be popular, he rejected the idea with the remark that he had never seen more than two people playing on each side of the net. That being so, he argued, there was obviously room for many more players and, as long as there was spare capacity on the existing court, there would be no need for a second.

During their first visit to St. Moritz, Lottie, Tony and Miss Legh, became friendly with Elizabeth Main and her current escort, Harold Topham.

A young widow who enjoyed a considerable reputation as a mountaineer, writer on mountaineering subjects, and photographer, Mrs. Main was later to become the first President of the Ladies' Alpine Club. Topham was an expert on the toboggan. He won the "Cresta Run Grand National" so often that he eventually retired in order not to win the challenge cup outright. He was also a holder of the St. Moritz Skating Award. In retrospect it seems clear that the relationship between Mrs. Main and Topham could not have been anything more than the passing one it proved to be: her whole life revolved about mountaineering; he found climbing a bore. Still, they were friendly enough when the Dod party met them.

Lottie and Tony took to mountaineering with enthusiasm. In company with Mrs. Main and a guide, Martin Schocher, they climbed the Zwei Schwestern on 13th February 1896.

On 19th February they made their second climb when they reached the summit of the Piz Zupo (4,002m). It was the first time that the mountain had been climbed in winter.

On the 23rd weather conditions were again suitable for climbing. Unfortunately for Lottie, however, she had sprained her wrist on the Cresta Run two days previously and was not fit to join the party. A reluctant Pennington Legh, who had refused to join the earlier expedition because she thought climbing dangerous, was persuaded to take her place. Her experiences on this particular day can have done nothing to dispel her original opinion. Indeed, had it not been for the skill of Martin Schocher, who the party had again hired, she might well have lost her life. She was following Schocher up a steep rock face on the Drei Blumen, with Tony behind her and Elizabeth Main bringing up the rear, when she lost her hold. Fortunately, the guide knew his job. Standing on a ledge above her, with the climbing rope belayed round a ledge of rock, he was able to arrest her fall, and then to haul her up to him, dangling like a sack of flour.

Switzerland, 19th February, 1896. Tony and Elizabeth Main climbing on Piz Zupo (13,000 feet).

1896 Lottie on the Cresta Run.

Understandably, when Lottie, Tony and Mrs. Main — once more with Schocher's professional assistance — completed their climbing for the season by scaling the 4,049 metres of the Piz Bernia in early March, Miss Legh was not with them.

In return for the instruction which they had received in tobogganning and climbing, Lottie and Tony helped Topham and Mrs. Main to improve their tennis.

Instead of returning home at the end of their Swiss holiday, Lottie, Tony, Elizabeth Main and Topham decided to make a cycling tour in Italy. Pennington Legh was invited to join the party, but was prevented from doing so by a previous engagement which demanded her returning to England.

The "1890's" was a period of cycling mania, and cycling tours were very fashionable. After decades of experiment and improvement, the bicycle had finally become a practicable vehicle, and many of those who could afford to do so took to the roads on it with enthusiasm. Some idea of the status enjoyed by the bicycle at that time may be gained from the fact that in 1896, when Annie won a golf competition, sponsored by *The Gentlewoman Magazine*, the first prize was a lady's bicycle, while the second was a gold bracelet.

Lottie had been interested in cycling since 1892, when she had visited some Irish friends who were keen cyclists. On that occasion a report in *The Irish Cyclist* had read: "Miss Lottie Dod, the champion lady tennis player, is at present sojourning at Portrush, indulging in the pastime of golf. She has learned to ride a safety, and is very keen on taking up cycling, and questioned us very closely on ladies' safeties generally and gears, tyres etc. in particular.

Miss Dod is the very picture of healthy, muscular, womanhood, brown as a berry, and with the regular athlete's eye. Whatever she takes up in the way of pastimes she means to excel at, and we feel sure she will make a crack rider." (21st September 1892).

Lottie, Tony, Elizabeth Main and Harry Topham travelled from Switzerland to Milan on the 13th March. After spending a few days there, they bought or hired the necessary bicycles, and then continued by train to Nervi, near Genoa, on the 18th.

Agreed that Rome should be their principal objective, they took to their bicycles on the 19th and, after riding by way of Rapallo, Spezia, Florence and Perugia, they arrived there on the 29th March.

After two weeks spent sightseeing, they left Rome on 12th April, and, travelling by way of Civita Castella and Gubbie, reached San Marino on the 19th. There they decided to finish their tour so that they would have time in hand to spend at the Italian Lakes and to see something of Switzerland in the spring, before coming home. It seems that at that point Lottie still intended to return to England in

Milan, 18th March 1896. Ready to set off on the cycling tour.
From left to right:
Harold Topham, Elizabeth Main, Lottie and Tony.

good time to practise for the Ladies' Union Golf Championship, which was arranged for the end of May.

In the course of some fourteen days actual cycling they had ridden more than five hundred miles. Considering the frequently difficult nature of the roads and the notoriously unreliable quality of the early pneumatic tyres, it was a very respectable achievement.

To a great extent it was made possible by the fact that they did not carry their own luggage. Instead, they sent it on ahead of them by local carriers from one hotel to the next. That they experienced no difficulty in this matter was probably due to their policy of paying handsomely, but only after seeing that their baggage had been delivered safely.

With two photographers in the party, the tour was well recorded and, from the evidence of Lottie's album, it is clear that they were fairly diligent tourists. They visited and photographed most of the popular attractions on their route, including the Carrara Quarries, Florence Cathedral, the Coliseum, and so on . . . Nude statues they invariably shot from a discreet angle — presumably because the pictures would eventually be inspected by Margaret Dod.

After completing their cycling tour the quartet lingered for several more weeks on the shores of, first the Italian, and then the Swiss, Lakes. In fact, they lingered for so long that by the time they returned to England it was too late for Lottie to enter the 1896 Ladies' Golf Championship.

Chapter Four

Lottie and Tony must have waxed lyrical about Switzerland because when they returned to St. Moritz in the following November their mother and Willy travelled with them.

Their arrival at the resort on the 17th was something of an anticlimax. Little snow had fallen, and the lake was unfrozen.

Still, there was always plenty to do at St. Moritz. While they waited for the snow and ice to appear the Dods spent their time playing tennis, walking, and renewing old acquaintances. Both Elizabeth Main and Harold Topham had returned to the "Kulm", so there were memories to be shared and plans to be made for the coming season.

They did not have to wait long for the onset of winter. A severe frost, which set in on the 20th, rendered the lake safe for skating by the 24th, and heavy snowfalls in late November and early December provided the necessary material for the reconstruction of the Cresta Run.

As might be expected, the new winter sports season followed much the same pattern as the previous one, with sport-filled days and convivial evenings for the visitors, and boom times for the Swiss locals.

Again the Dods tried the full range of sporting possibilities.

Willy found a particular interest in curling and, with the remarkable Dod aptitude for sport, soon began to show much

16th January, 1897. St. Moritz. Lottie skates to pass the Men's Test.

promise. It was the beginning of a life-long interest. At that time the standard of curling was nowhere higher than at St. Moritz, and in the pre-Great War years Willy returned to the resort season after season to enjoy the sport. Even after the War, and as late as the '1930's', he continued to make occasional visits to St. Moritz.

Almost as soon as skating was possible Lottie began to prepare for the very demanding Men's Skating Test. Over the following weeks she devoted two hours a day to training, under the guidance of Harold Topham, and, on the 16th January, 1987, she passed the Test, thereby becoming the second woman to do so.

To suit Margaret, the Family returned to England shortly afterwards. No traveller and no socialite, she had grown tired of the snow and the incessant junketings of the resort.

Because they were obliged to return home before the beginning of the mountaineering season, the Dods did no climbing in Switzerland that year, but before they left St. Moritz, Lottie and Tony agreed to accompany Elizabeth Main on a climbing tour in Norway during the following summer.

An account of their adventures in Norway was written by Mrs. Main and published over a year later as a two-part feature in *The Queen, The Lady's Newspaper*, issues dated 22nd and 29th October, 1898.

As Elizabeth Main was the only member of the party who could be regarded as fully-experienced climber, and as none of them had been to Norway before, they took the precaution of engaging the services of a well-known Swiss guide, one Joseph Imboden, described by Mrs. Main in the following terms.

". . . . we may say that he is past middle age, but does not look it; has a temper quickly tried by stupidity in his associates, but does not show it; has a magnificent knowledge of his work . . . and is our most devoted philosopher and friend in every circumstance which may arise."

The expense incurred in securing Imboden's services proved to have been well worth-while, the local guides they engaged doing nothing to capture Elizabeth Main's confidence. The Norwegian guides, she alleged, all shared three well-marked characteristics: they had no nails in their boots; they refused to deviate from their usual routes; and they were inclined either to leave the climbing rope so slack that it caught round every projection, or jerk on the rope in a peremptory and very unpleasant manner. On many occasions Imboden's superb mountaincraft helped to reduce the distances they would otherwise have been obliged to walk and to increase the comfort and safety of the climbs.

They sailed from Hull to Bergen in July 1897. From Bergen they travelled by coastal steamer to Skjolden at the head of the Sogne

Fiord, with the intention of climbing some of the peaks in the Horunger Range. At Sulheim's Hotel they rested for a day, eating raspberries and red-currants in the garden and gazing out over the sunlit Fiord, activities that seem to have reflected a social and recreational provision superior to that found at most of the hotels where they were to stay during their tour, before they started on the four hour walk to the Turtegroe Hotel at the foot of the mountains.

With breathtaking presumption, the first peak they decided to climb was the 2,405 metre Skagastolstind, which was said to be the hardest ascent in Norway, and considerable more difficult than the Matterhorn.

Having been assured at their hotel that the mountain hut on the lower slopes of Skagastolstind was well-equipped, they set out in bright sunshine with the intention of staying the night there before making their assault on the Peak.

Throughout their stay in Norway they climbed in an order suggested by Imboden, unless some particular local difficulty demanded a temporary change in the arrangement. The Swiss guide himself led the way, followed by Lottie. Next came the local guide and, behind him, Elizabeth Main. Tony brought up the rear, recording times and heights, with watch and aneroid, and carrying great loads of cameras, wraps, bottles and wines, and bars of chocolate, all jumbled together in his enormous Zermatt knapsack. As they had done in Italy, both Elizabeth and Tony captured the highlights of the tour on photographic plates.

They discovered that the hotel manager had exaggerated the conveniences of the hut. Its fittings consisted of three dirty cups, a kettle without a lid or spout, and old meat tin, some rugs "of which only the holes remained", and a few blankets. The beds consisted of two six-inch wide planks.

Encouraged by the permanent residents of the blankets, they rose early the next morning to find heavy rain falling and the peak above them hidden by cloud.

Disappointed, but undeterred, they pressed on with the climb after breakfast. Despite the unfavourable weather, they were able to make good progress because the route they used was both sheltered and direct. They narrowly avoided a possible disaster when Imboden noticed that a length of rope fitted in a chimney near the top of the mountain for the convenience of climbers was rotten, and reached the summit in about three and a half hours.

According to Elizabeth, Lottie "went like a bird, and gazed into space with the steady eye and untrembling nerve of an eagle."

The continuance of bad weather at Turtegroe disrupted their plans for further ascents in the Horunger, and they decided to move to the other area on their itinerary, the Romsdal valley.

July 1897, Norway. Hotel at Skjolden. Lottie, Elizabeth Main and their Swiss guide, Joseph Imboden.

2nd August, 1897, Norway. Mountain hut on lower slopes of Skagastolstind (2,405 metres). Lottie with Swiss guide Joseph Imboden (smoking) and local guide.

To avoid the sea journey down the Sognfiord, northwards along the coast and then up the Nordfiord, they travelled from Skjolden to Marifjaeren by ferry, and then drove northwards up the Jostedal Valley to Faeberg. There they hired two porters to carry their luggage on the next leg of the journey, which involved the crossing of the great Jostedalsbreen ice field on foot.

They set out to cross the glacier on a hot morning, but, as they approached it, the weather began to deteriorate. "After we had walked for about four and a half hours to the foot of the glacier the weather became abominable and Imboden said, very decidedly, that if it got any worse he would simply turn back . . . Down came the rain in rivers, and we looked a sad-faced gang as we filed along up the huge glacier, the splendid tributaries of which we could dimly see, trembling in blue seracs, out of the mist to our left. After a couple of hours more, some rocks were seen to our right, while ahead our glacier rose in a series of complicated crevasses to a high, snowy, saddle, doubtless the pass. Imboden instinctively made for the rocks by which were were to outflank the ice-fall and he proved to be right. Our dripping party mounted up some way over stones, and then tried, with praiseworthy success, to make merry over a meal, considerably cheered by the certainty that there was now no chance of our turning back, and that the pass was but a quarter of an hour distant. Our deep regret, however, was that we could see so little of the view for the glimpses that we had obtained were a revelation as to glacier scenery in Norway. A tramp over a level snow field succeeded the rocks and before long the mist thinned out, the sun struggled through, and we rejoiced in the promise of a fine afternoon. The descent of the glacier was easy, and we could see below a narrow valley, a mere rift in the mountains, towards which the icy stream was taking us . . ."

Crossing the Jostedalsbreen — a distance of about 25 miles — occupied some fourteen hours.

They finished their trek at Hjele on the Lake of Stryn. There they stayed for the night, and then continued their northwards journey to Oje in the Romsdal Valley in a hired open carriage driven by Lottie.

During the fortnight the Party spent in the Romsdal Valley they climbed many of the area's most challenging peaks, including Slogan, Mjolnir, Vengatind and the Romsdalshorn, assisted by a settled spell of very fine weather. Climbing the 1,550 metre Romsdalshorn and the 1,852 metre Vengatind afforded Lottie and Elizabeth the special satisfaction of being the first women to make the ascents.

The descent of the last mountain they climbed on the tour, the 2,000 metre Mjolnir, was enlivened by a rather dramatic incident. They had stopped for lunch at a place that they believed to be safe, when a rock, loosened from the glacier above them by the sun,

Norway 1897. The Party (with Lottie driving) approaches the Vengetind (6,000 metres). Lottie and Elizabeth Main became the first ladies to climb this peak on 16th August, 1897.

Norway, 1897. Climbing on the Mjohnir. Tony, Lottie, Imboden and local guide.

hurtled down directly towards them. The local guide saw it first and shouted a warning. Imboden whose back had been towards it, awoke to the danger and flung himself between the rock and Elizabeth. A split second later, the rock struck a boulder and was smashed into a multitude of fragments, which flew past their heads like grapeshot. Amazingly, none of them was even scratched.

Elizabeth concluded her account of the tour: "From what we have seen of climbing in Norway, we do not think that many people would care, now that all the more important peaks have been ascended, to return to the recognised mountaineering centres year after year. The climbing is much inferior to that obtainable in Switzerland, the scenery in the heights is comparatively tame, the discomforts are greater, and the weather more uncertain. In short, we feel that we have climbed a little in Norway, and we have thoroughly enjoyed our trip, but we do not wish to make another in the same country for the purposes of mountaineering."

In the event, Elizabeth was to reconsider this decision and make several more climbing visits to Norway.

Not so Lóttie. For her, the end of the trip appears to have marked the end of her interest in mountaineering. If she did climb again, no record of the event now exists.

This was to become typical of her. Once her interest in a particular sport had been worked out, she immediately dropped that sport, sometimes with an almost startling abruptness.

In the case of mountaineering however, there was an additional reason: at some time in 1898 she quarreled with her climbing mentor Elizabeth Main. During the summer of that year she and Tony again joined forces with Elizabeth to cruise the Norwegian coast and the Lofoten Islands, and it seems likely that the rift occurred during the long days and weeks they spent at sea.

Just what they quarreled about is no longer known, but their differences were so bitter that they were never resolved. When Elizabeth wrote her book *Mountaineering in the Land of the Midnight Sun* (Published by Fisher Unwin 1908) she made no mention of Lottie or Tony by name. The nearest she approached was:

"The first time I visited Norway was in 1897. We were in a party of four, including Joseph Imboden, and on that occasion we restricted ourselves to the south."

Nor had she become any more forgiving twenty years later and thirty years after the event when, under her later married name of Le Blond, she wrote her autobiography *Day in Day out* (Published by Lane 1928). Indeed, in her determination to avoid all reference to the Dods, she descended to lying. For example, according to her account of the episode, she made the 1896 cycling tour alone.

Chapter Five

In 1897 Lottie became interested in (what was for women) the newly-emergent game of hockey. So novel was the idea of women playing hockey that some players were taunted in the streets as "unsexed creatures", and the few publications that included match reports did so in an intermittent, haphazard, almost hesitant manner, rendering a close reconstruction of Lottie's hockey-playing career difficult.

It is, however, a matter of historical fact that the formation of "The Ladies' Hockey Association" in 1895 (the title was changed in 1896 to "The All England Women's Hockey Association") was followed by a rapid increase in the number of women's colleges and girls' schools adopting hockey, and by the founding of many women's hockey clubs and county associations.

Just where and how Lottie learned to play is no longer known. It is clear, however, that in 1897 she helped to found a ladies' hockey club at Spital — a mile or so from "Edgeworth" — and that by 1899 she had been playing well enough to have been appointed Club Captain and Captain of the Cheshire County Team, and to have been chosen to play for England.

She was also very active in working to promote the interests of the game off the field. In 1898 she was appointed to represent Spital Club on the first Committee of the Northern Ladies Hockey Association (later to become The Northern Counties Women's Hockey Association), which met at Manchester, and from 1899 to 1901 she served as President of the Northern Association. She represented the North on the Executive of the All England Women's Hockey Association during her Presidency, and she is known to have made an effective contribution to the defeat of a motion, sponsored by the South, which would have amalgamated the Northern and Midland Associations.

On the field Lottie's usual place was at centre-forward. From the few accounts of the Club's matches at this period which have survived it appears that when Lottie played Spital won and when she was absent it lost.

In October 1898 she led the Cheshire team to a 4-1 victory over Lancashire at Blundellsands, scoring all four Cheshire goals in a match that was principally noteworthy for being played in torrential rain.

Five months later the *Liverpool Echo* reported, "The return match took place at Spital, when the home team again proved their superiority, beating Lancashire 11 goals to 1, a defeat all the more terrible as Lancashire was considered to have a better team than when they last played, while Cheshire had to make some alterations in their eleven. Six goals were shot by Miss Dod."

On 21st March 1899 Lottie played at inside-right for the England team which beat Ireland 3-1 at Richmond Athletic Ground.

The correspondent of *The Gentlewomen* appears to have found the match itself disappointing, describing it as "one-sided" but she was enthusiastic about the prowess of certain individual players.

"Although Miss Dod is somewhat behind the others in the matter of pace," she wrote, "she is surprisingly quick and powerful in her strokes and exceedingly tricky in dribbling and passing. She is a very strong player."

Lottie had to wait for a year before she again appeared in an international — the Scottish and Welsh Associations had yet to be formed — but, in the meantime, she played in a number of interesting club and county matches.

In February 1900 she captained and played at centre-forward for the Northern Association when it beat the South 6-2 at Knutsford.

"Throughout the match Miss Dod showed herself to be a brilliant shot and a hard-working centre," reported the *Liverpool Echo*.

No doubt, if there were any southern diehards who had continued to advocate a merger of the other two associations after the decision of the National Executive, that result gave them food for thought.

In March 1900 Lottie played for England a second time, on that occasion at centre-forward, in the team which beat Ireland by two goals to one at Ballsbridge, Dublin. Although it is known that both English goals were scored by Lottie, no record of the match appears to exist.

Later in the same year Lottie was chosen to play centre-forward for England in their first fixture against Wales, but she was prevented from doing so by an attack of sciatica.

It was the first onslaught of an affliction that was to trouble her at irregular intervals for the remainder of her life. Some bouts were so severe that they prostrated her, and rendered any sport impossible for months; other, milder, attacks, constituted a serious handicap when she played in important events.

Even so, Lottie never attempted to minimise any defeat or detract from any opponent's triumph by mentioning that she had been suffering from sciatica. Indeed, she managed to conceal the fact that she was subject to such attacks so successfully that it never became public knowledge during her lifetime. It now seems very probably that on those occasions when she had played far below her best form and sports writers had been obliged to speculate on the reason for it, she had been suffering from sciatica.

February, 1900. The Northern Hockey Team which beat the South 6-2.

That first attack was both severe and prolonged, confining Lottie to her bed for several weeks and preventing her from playing in major sporting events for many months.

In the event, the England team did not seem to miss Lottie too much: they defeated Wales by thirteen goals to nil.

By the summer of 1901 she had recovered sufficiently to travel to Ireland and see Willy win the South of Ireland Golf Championship but, before she could return to the public arena, her mother fell ill, and, on 1st August 1901, Margaret Dod died.

As a mark of respect, the Family played in no competitions for the remainder of the year and, by the time that Lottie was able to resume her sporting activities she appears to have lost interest in hockey. She resigned from the Northern Committee and, although from time to time she turned out for Spital until she left Cheshire in 1905, she never again played hockey for county or country.

Chapter Six

Lottie began to play golf when she was fifteen. That is, in the same year that she won her first Wimbledon title.

Although there was at the time no golf club on the Wirral Peninsula — and very few elsewhere — that would admit women, both Willy and Tony were members of The Royal Liverpool Club at Hoylake, and it was on that course, and as her brothers' guest, that Lottie took her first lessons from the Professional, Jack Morris.

There is no doubt that, of all the sports in which she achieved international standing, Lottie found golf to be the most demanding, and she did not acquire its skills without difficulty. For some years after she had begun to play it was only with an almost obvious effort that she managed to control a tendency to slice the ball when driving.

For all that, golf presented a challenge that she enjoyed. Indeed, she once wrote that the greatest pleasure of any sport is to be found in learning to play it.

Determined to overcome her problems, Lottie made the twenty-mile round trip from Bebington to Hoylake and back in the Family's horse-drawn trap, whenever one or both of her brothers went to play — often three or four times a week. In addition, she spent long hours practising on the putting green that Tony and Willy had laid out at "Edgeworth", and she attended as many major tournaments as possible to study the top men players in action.

In the later "1880s" and early 1890s" there was little possibility of gauging the standard of the best women players because there was then no such thing as a major women's golf tournament.

A growing interest in the Game on the part of many women, with its attendant demands for a general acceptance of women's golf, was met by much male opposition. From the "1860s" most clubs had allowed women to accompany their menfolk to courses, but they were then expected to potter about on a small putting green while their husbands or brothers played serious golf. The idea of their playing on the sacred turf of the actual courses was enough to provoke the more reactionary men to fury. It was claimed that women were too weak and slow to play properly, and that their incessant chatter would unsettle the men. By the standards of the time, in allowing Lottie to play golf with her brothers, the Committee of The Royal Liverpool Golf Club was demonstrating a remarkably enlightened attitude.

Royal Portrush was another liberal-minded club, actually organising tournaments for ladies and for mixed couples. It was there in September, 1892, that Lottie first tried her golfing skills in an open competition, entering and winning the mixed foursomes in partnership with Willy.

Happily for Lottie — and those like her — in the years when she was learning to play, the position of women's golf had begun to improve rapidly. Some of the more spirited women players had started to found separate women's clubs, and, early in 1893, twenty of these clubs co-operated to establish the Ladies Golf Union as the governing body for the women's game. More than any other single event, it was the formation of the L.G.U. that marked the beginning of women's golf as a serious sport.

The first act of the new body was to introduce a national championship, with prizes of: a trophy worth £50, to be held by the winner's club for a year; a gold medal for the winner; a silver medal for the runner-up; and bronze medals for the losing semi-finalists. It was primarily in competition for this Championship that the standard of the top women players was raised out of all recognition in the course of the following ten years or so.

When the first L.G.U. tournament was held at Lytham and St. Anne's in May 1893, Lottie was a spectator in the crowd which followed the play and saw Lady Margaret Scott emerge as the first national ladies' champion.

In February, 1894 she became a founder member of a new ladies' club at Moreton, a few miles from Hoylake.

Carved from a desolate stretch of scrubland, the course was never more than adequate, but the atmosphere of the Club itself seems to have been warm and friendly. Much emphasis was placed on foursomes, and, on match days, the interior of the wooden pavilion-type clubhouse was always brightly decorated with flowers and bunting, and a sumptuous lunch was served.

Although it was a small club and destined to survive for a mere twenty years or so — until, in fact, the course disappeared under the plough during the First World War — Moreton Ladies secured an honourably place in the annals of women's golf by producing two national champions.

It was as founder members that Lottie and Molly Graham met. They became good friends and, in the years that followed, often travelled together to the various tournaments in which they played.

Sister of Jack Graham — still widely regarded as the finest player who failed to win the Amateur Championship — Molly Graham exercised a fluent command over the complete range of strokes, and combined in her personality a vigorously competitive spirit with an unassuming manner. Like Lottie, she was an all-rounder. Although her first interest was in golf, she played a good standard of badminton and tennis, and she was an enthusiastic climber.

Having studied the competitors at Lytham and St. Annes, Lottie concluded that her own game had reached a standard where she would not be disgraced if she entered the 1894 Championship, to be held at Littlestone in Kent. News of her entry prompted one sports journalist to write:

"Now Lottie Dod, so neatly shod
Steps forth upon the tee
On tennis green she is the Queen
At Golf what will she be?"

In the event, she reached the third round before she was eliminated. The Championship was again won by Lady Margaret Scott.

Of the competition itself the golf correspondent of *Ladies Realm* was able to observe:

". . . . what a change was visible in the golf all round! — indisputably a marked improvement since the previous year; for now ladies were, with their drivers and irons, carrying (and fairly easily, too) hazards that before would have been considered too much for any woman, or making creditable shots out of Sahara — like bunkers, and fine putts on those billiard-table greens, showing that already the Championship was doing its work of improving the play through painstaking observation and experience."

1895 Portsalon Golf Links, Co. Denegal. A foursome. Lottie and Tony play two unknown men opponents. Lottie watches while Tony marks the cup for one of their opponents.

The fact was, women's golf was entering a boom period. In 1895 Walter Dalrymple, editor of *Golfers' Guide* noted that there were then seventy to eighty ladies' clubs in the country.

Between Littlestone and the 1895 Championship Tournament at Portrush, Lottie travelled the length and breadth of the country to play in as many tournaments as she could.

At Portrush she caused a stir by defeating the formidable Sybil Whingham, 2 and 1, in the third round.

Hearth and Home commented,
"Miss Sybil Whingham, a lady who has been playing since childhood, and who created much sensation by her brilliant driving in the competition was beaten by Miss Dod, the ex-tennis champion. Miss Dod is steady and she plays with her head."(30th May, 1895)

Lottie's play was impressive enough to convince some observers that here, at last, was a player capable of beating Lady Margaret. They were mistaken. When she met the champion in the fourth round Lottie succumbed by three down and two to play. For the third, and last, time before she retired from competition golf, Lady Margaret won the trophy.

When Lady Margaret Scott announced her retirement there were many who regarded Lottie as her most likely successor. *The Scotsman* described her style as businesslike:

" 'When unadorned, adorned the most,' was never more applicable to any lady's play. There is no mannerism about it. Some ladies spend almost as much time over their putting as they do over their morning toilet. Not so Miss Dod. With her there is no haste, no undue pressure, no apparent nervous anxiety. Due thought is given at every stroke to distance, lie, and the proper club to be used, yet there is an utter absence of anything approaching ostentation."

Lottie did not compete in the 1896 Tournament, having lingered too long in Switzerland at the end of her Italian-Swiss tour. By not returning in time to play, Lottie sacrificed the best opportunity of winning the title which had so far presented itself to her: the 1896 L.G.U. Championship was held on The Royal Liverpool Course at Hoylake, the course where she had learned to play golf, and where she might have expected to start with some advantage over most of the other competitors. That she was prepared to forgo such an opportunity seems a clear indication that she had found the Swiss interlude particularly enjoyable.

She did play the following year, when the event was held at Gullane in Scotland, but without distinction. In 1898 she again played in the Championship at Great Yarmouth and, in the face of a half-gale that scoured the faces of competitors, officials, and spectators with sand from the beach, she won through to the semi-final. There she was defeated by Miss E. Neville on the last green.

By 1899, when she was beaten in the fifth round by May Hezlet who went on to win the title, Lottie's chances of winning the event appeared to have passed. Miss Hezlet was one of a new, gifted, generation of women golfers, who looked set to dominate the game for years to come.

Even so, Lottie was still considered to be an automatic choice when an English team was selected to meet an Irish team in an unofficial international match at Newcastle, County Down, in the same year. There she justified her place in the team by beating her opponent, Miss Magill 9-0, and the English team went on to win the event 37-18.

The match was unofficial because there was, at the time, no administrative machinery to regulate international women's golf matches. It was a deficiency that Lottie thought should be rectified, and over the course of the next few years she pressed the need for a properly constituted body to promote and govern home internationals whenever she had access to an influential ear.

L.G.U. Golf Championship. Deal, 1902. Fourth round.

In 1900 she again reached the semi-final of the L.G.U. Championship, held that year at Westward Ho!, before she was defeated by Mrs. Wilson Hoare by one hole.

When women's county golf was introduced in 1899/1900 the Cheshire selectors invited Lottie to captain the county team, but the idea was novel and regarded with suspicion by many suitable players. Like several other counties, Cheshire could not raise a team, and was, therefore, obliged to drop out of the competition before a single game had been played.

1901 was the year in which Lottie played no competitive sport, being prostrated by sciatica for several months in the first half of the year, and being in mourning for her mother during the second half.

As far as golf was concerned, however, there was some consolation for her, and much joy for Moreton Ladies Club when Molly Graham won the L.G.U. Championship at Aberdovey.

Next year Lottie again entered the Championship, which was played at Deal. Despite her lack of recent big match play, she won her way through to the fifth round before being trounced by Sybil Whingham, 7 up and 5 to play.

Lottie did not play in the 1903 Championship Tournament, but at Troon in 1904 she returned to make another challenge.

The years between early 1901 and early 1904 was the one period in Lottie's long career as a top athlete during which the Press grew indifferent to her and, when the Championship opened on 10th May, there were few commentators who were prepared to regard her as a potential winner of a competition that included two brilliant young players in the persons of Rhona Adair and May Hezlet. Miss Adair was the current holder of the title and she and May Hezlet had each won two of the previous five competitions.

Possibly it was the general obsession with Adair and Hezlet; possibly it was the very large field of sixty-two competitors; possibly it was the cold, wet windy weather which inhibited journalists from straying far from the comforts of the nineteenth hole for any length of time, but, whatever the reason, it was not until the fifth round that the reporters turned their attention to Lottie.

By that time the overall match situation had simplified: Hezlet had eliminated Adair in the fourth round, the number of competitors had been reduced to eight, and the weather had moderated a little. With fewer variables to occupy them, a number of journalists suddenly noticed that Lottie was playing superb golf.

In the fifth round she defeated her old rival Sybil Whingham, 2 and 1, thereby gaining her revenge for the 1902 result, and qualifying for the semi-final.

L.G.U. Championship. Deal, 1902. Fifth round. Sybil Whingham watches Lottie putt.

Moreton Ladies were represented by two members in the competition and, remarkably, they both won through to the semi-finals. In one match Lottie faced Dorothy Campbell, while in the other Molly Graham played May Hezlet. Lottie beat Miss Campbell by four holes up and two to play but Molly succumbed to May Hezlet.

Despite the squally weather a crowd of some 4,000 to 5,000 spectators gathered to see the final on the afternoon of 13th May. It was, in fact, the biggest crowd to have attended any L.G.U. final to that date, regular golfing enthusiasts being reinforced by a large number of shipyard workers, who had taken a holiday, and a large number of school children who the official L.G.U. records scathingly describe as having been "turned loose". It was also a crowd that was in a high state of noisy excitement long before the players walked out to the first tee.

In the event, the spectators' expectations were fully justified. The match could not have been more closely fought. Both women were dogged competitors, and from the first drive nothing was given away.

At an early stage in the game it became clear that it was to be a contest between Miss Hezlet's inspired driving and iron play, and Lottie's powers of recovery and brilliant putting.

Against all predictions Lottie secured an early lead by winning the first hole and then, to the delight of her many supporters, grimly hung on to it. Try as she might, it seemed that May Hezlet would not be able to draw even. They played shot for shot until they reached the fifteenth where a particularly fine iron shot on to the green enabled May Hezlet to win the hole and draw level with her opponent. She then went on to win the sixteenth.

For the first time in the game the crowd fell completely silent. At one down and two to play Lottie was staring defeat in the face.

Typically, she kept her nerve and went on to win the seventeenth.

It was all too much for the spectators. Their excitement boiled over into a frenzied uproar of cheering and counter-cheering, jostling and jeering, that brought play to a halt.

The stewards appealed for order, but it was not for several minutes and not until the captain of Troon Club, William Law, had announced that the match would be abandoned unless the spectators behaved in a seemly manner, that the players were able to continue.

During the disturbance Lottie remained completely calm and, noticing that May Hezlet appeared to be somewhat apprehensive, she walked over to her and chatted reassuringly until the crisis — for such it seemed to all present — had passed.

The last hole was played in an almost uncanny silence, as if spectators, officials and players were holding their collective breaths. The hole, and the match, was decided on the home green, when May Hezlet missed a long putt by a hair's breadth, while Lottie sank hers.

At the same moment that the winning ball rattled in the cup the crowd began to surge forward as if to engulf the players, but the stewards were too quick for them. Without hesitation, they seized the two women by the arms and bundled them to the safety of the clubhouse.

By winning the L.G.U. title, Lottie became the only woman to win both the British Tennis and Golf Championships.

"Her victory was no surprise," commented *The Scotsman* which had not made any previous mention of her. "There were others who undoubtedly caught popular fancy to a greater degree, such as Miss Adair, Miss May Hezlet and Miss Glover, but Miss Dod's past record in the annual tournament was too well-known to gain her other than a high place in the estimation of those versed in matters relating to ladies' golf." (17th May, 1904)

Others, too, were wise with the benefit of hindsight.

"It was at Littlestone that Miss Dod, like so many other players of mark, made her first appearance in public as a golfer. How well one remembers the comments, although it is ten years ago, how vividly one recalls the opinions expressed in no measured terms that Miss

63

Troon. 13th May, 1904. Lottie, the new British Ladies' Golf Champion, May Hezlet, runner-up, and Dorothy Campbell and Molly Graham, semi-finalists.

Dod would assuredly one day be lady champion at golf as well as at tennis." (Golfing 23rd February, 1905)

Once more the Press was at Lottie's feet. Never again would it desert her.

Among the flood of congratulatory messages and invitations that arrived at "Edgeworth" as a result of Lottie's triumph was one from the former American Ladies' Champion, Frances Griscom, inviting Lottie to attend the 1904 American Championship as an observer. and to stay at Miss Griscom's Philadelphia home during her visit.

Frances Griscom was a long-standing friend, and Lottie replied to the effect that she would be delighted to accept her invitation, with the opportunities if would afford of meeting Frances again and of seeing the top American women golfers in action.

On 21st September she sailed from Liverpool on the American line ship "Merion" — by something of a coincidence a ship which bore the same name as the Club where the American Ladies' Championship was to be held — and arrived at New York on 2nd October. There she was met by Miss Griscom, with an invitation to compete in the Championship, an invitation which came as a complete surprise to Lottie because it represented a change in the rules. The rule which had previously restricted entry to American citizens had been changed to allow others to compete, and it had been changed for Lottie's particular benefit.

Fortunately, she had taken her clubs with her, and on the following day she began her training by playing in a tournament at Miss Griscom's Club, The Riverton Country, from which she emerged as the winner.

A reporter from the Philadelphia *Morning Ledger,* who was sent to the Griscom home to interview Lottie, described her return from the tournament.

"Miss Griscom and her guest arrived back at 'Dolobran' at about 6 o'clock, and, as they came into the library the former American Champion pointed to the cup Miss Dod was carrying and said laughingly,

'You see, she has started in already.'

'Yes, and it was so pleasant to play against your American women,' said Miss Dod. 'They are certainly good sportswomen, and I am delighted to think I have been asked to play in the national tournament. I did not know I was going to play, but simply came to watch it. But I understand that they have invited me in return for your magnificent player Mr. Travis being asked to play in the English Tournament.' " (4th October 1904)

As always when she was talking to a reporter, Lottie had obviously kept her verbal guard well up. On this occasion the journalist was allowed to linger, but he added nothing of substance to his report except that Lottie was "a charming conversationalist".

Next day Lottie and Frances won the Riverton Club Scotch Foursomes Tournament.

Unhappily, Lottie's performance in the American Ladies' Tournament, which was held at the Merion Club, Haverford, was the worst of her life in a major golf event.

Having — not without difficulty — qualified in the preliminary round, she was beaten in the first round by Pauline MacKay, who was rated no more than a good player.

At once *The Morning Ledger* rushed to her defence. "Without the slightest wish to detract from the young Bostonian's victory, there can be no question that Miss Dod was far from being on her game.

She had come prepared for raw, searching, weather, instead of which she was confronted with an enervating and stifling air which must have afflicted her. Throughout the game she never seemed able to buckle down to the task before her and played her shots with a lack of the confidence necessary in an important struggle."

The British papers adopted a similar attitude.

"It was perfectly evident throughout," commented *Golf,* "that Miss Dod was not playing her game, and some spectators who had seen her win at Troon said she was about half a stroke worse. The reason is not hard to seek, apart from the fact that she was playing among strange surroundings, the clay at Merion had been baked hard and dry so that it was quite impossible to play through the green in the same way as would be done in England or Scotland. At Merion the ball had to be hit clean, for an iron or brassey on Merion turf would merely slide along the fair green as if frozen."

Disappointing as this first appearance of a Briton in their Championship Tournament had been, the Americans expressed their appreciation of Lottie's entry by presenting her with a handsome and very heavy silver tray.

While she was in the United States Lottie tried to persuade as many of the leading women golfers as she met there to enter for the 1905 British Tournament. Finding that the suggestion provoked considerable interest, she raised the matter with the L.G.U. when she returned to the United Kingdom in November. The Union welcomed the idea and changed the rules to allow foreign entries for the Tournament.

During Lottie's absence the L.G.U. had appointed a committee to establish the administrative machinery to govern an international competition between the home countries — a subject of long-standing interest to Lottie — and on her return she was invited to serve on it. This committee worked to such good effect that the first competition was arranged for the following May.

Possibly encouraged by Lottie's triumph at Troon, the Cheshire Ladies' Golf Committee decided to make another attempt to raise a county team. This time they were successful and, in the spring of 1905, Cheshire Ladies, under Lottie's captaincy, played two matches. They lost the first at Ilkley, despite Lottie beating the Yorkshire Captain, Evelyn Steele, by 6 and 4, but they beat Lancashire in a match held at Hoylake, when Lottie defeated her opponent, Maude Buckley, by 7 and 6.

Late May 1905 brought to Cromer the greatest women's golf jamboree that this country had seen. Crowded into the few days between 25th May and 2nd June were the first (unofficial) international between the United Kingdom and the United States, the first official home international tournament between England, Ireland, and Scotland, and the L.G.U. Championship competition.

It was a situation that presented Lottie with the daunting challenge of playing in three internationals and the national championship in the course of a week or so. Other top players were faced with a similar task, but they did not have to bear the additional burdens of captaining the British and English teams and of being defending champion.

That Lottie herself was at least partly responsible for this apparently unreasonable situation seems clear. As a member of the Home Internationals Committee, she must have been involved in planning the home internationals, including the decisions concerning dates and venues. There was, however, much to be said for arranging for the home internationals to be held at the same place and within a few days of the L.G.U. Tournament: first, the top British players who would gather at Cromer for the Championship would not have to travel elsewhere or to find a space in their diaries for the internationals and might, therefore, be more easily induced to play in them, and, secondly, the enthusiasts who travelled to see the Championship might also attend the internationals with a resultant increase in receipts and publicity.

The British-American match appears to have been arranged at short notice when the number and calibre of the American players who arrived at Cromer to compete in the Championship was known, and it was fixed for the 25th May, the day before the first of the home internationals.

Lottie agreed to captain the seven player British team, which included a number of women whose names have passed into golfing legend. There was May Hezlet, who had already won the British Championship twice and was destined to win it again in 1907; Dorothy Campbell, who was to become the first player to win both the British and American Championships; Molly Graham, winner of the British Championship in 1901, and three others of scarcely inferior prowess. The American team, too, looked strong. Captained by the United States' Champion, Georgina Bishop, it included two future American Champions in the persons of Harriet and Margaret Curtis.

Disappointingly for Lottie, she was the only Briton to loose her match, but not before she had engaged Georgina Bishop in a struggle of Homeric intensity. "Both Miss Bishop and Miss Dod played a good long game," reported *The Times*, "but they were equally weak in approaching and putting. Miss Bishop was three holes down at the turn, but was "all square" at the end of the round and won on the 20th green." (26th May, 1905).

That first British-American, match was to make a lasting impression on international women's golf.

The Curtis sisters enjoyed the contest so much that they conceived the idea of having regular international fixtures, but it was not until 1932 when the biennial matches between representatives of the U.S.A. and the British Isles were established, that their vision became a reality.

On the day following the British-American match, England was defeated by Scotland 4-3, with Lottie losing to Molly Graham, who was playing for Scotland by virtue of her Scottish parentage.

In the England-Ireland match, played on the 28th, Lottie faced May Hezlet for the first time since she defeated her in the previous year's Championship Tournament.

"Miss M. Hezlet started badly by foozling her drive, but she holed a long putt for a three on the first green and, after standing "all square" at the turn, she beat Miss Dod at the 17th hole." (Times — 29th May).

Possibly Lottie gleaned some consolation from the English 4-3 victory.

Such, then, was Lottie's gruelling and disheartening preparation for the Championship, an event that had attracted a record number of 137 entries.

When the contest began, on 30th May, it soon became evident that Lottie was playing well below her best form. She won her way through the first three rounds, but she was defeated 4-3 in the fourth by Bertha Thompson — somewhat ironically because it was in the fourth round of the previous year's Championship that Lottie had eliminated Bertha Thompson, and, just as Lottie had done in 1904, Miss Thompson went on to win the title.

As usual, the Press rushed to offer Lottie its sympathy.

"It was unfortunate that last year's Champion, Miss Dod, was not playing her best game, but she was only defeated by Miss Thompson in the fourth heat on the sixteenth green, and will, no doubt, be in better form next year." (*Country Life 10th June*).

The writer might have added that none of those who had played for Britain in the British-American encounter — widely regarded as the seven most gifted women golfers in the Kingdom — had reached the Championship Final. Without doubt, the effort of playing in the trans-Atlantic match, the Home Internationals, and the Championship itself, in the space of a week had taken its toll.

As far as Lottie was concerned "next year" never came. In the months that followed the Cromer Tournament her enthusiasm for golf was displaced by a new interest: archery.

Chapter Seven

In the Autumn of 1905 Lottie and her brothers sold "Edgeworth" and moved to a large house on the outskirts of Newbury, Berkshire. This they re-named "Edgecombe" to conform with Dod family tradition.

Their main reason for moving to Newbury seems to have been a wish to live closer to Annie and her family, but not so close that they no longer lived in the countryside.

After their wedding in 1889 Annie and Ernest Worssam had set up home at 10 Finsbury Circus, London. There a daughter, Doris, had been born in 1890, followed by two sons, Ray and Geoffrey, who were born in 1901 and 1902 respectively.

Despite her domestic duties and the obligations of motherhood — both of which she took seriously — Annie had maintained an active interest in sports and games of all kinds.

A fine golfer, she played regularly for Middlesex in the years around the turn of the century and was, at one time, a member of five clubs. Although her ambition to play on every course in the country seems to have been unfulfilled, she compiled a list which shows that she played on at least seventy-seven of them.

Billiards was another of her interests. Encouraged by her husband, Annie learned to play the game to such good effect that, according to a glossy magazine published on 14th March, 1908, she was the best woman player in the country at that time. The article was accompanied by a picture of Annie posing at the billiards table, head up for the benefit of the photographer, bearing the caption "The amateur lady champion of billiards". Unfortunately, the page has been preserved, but the remainder of the magazine was thrown away and it is now impossible to identify it.

Such was the Worssams' enthusiasm for billiards that they arranged for electricty to be installed in their home during the early "1890's" for the sole purpose of illuminating the billiards table.

Annie was also an enthusiastic archer, practising with the Royal Toxophilite Society at Regents' Park. Although the Society did not, at that time, admit women as members — and did not do so until 1924 — it afforded them access to its facilities and promoted a prestigious annual "Ladies' Day" meeting.

Lottie, Willy and Tony had practised archery for some years at "Edgeworth" and at Lyme Hall, Cheshire, coached by the Legh family. They could have found no better mentors. Piers Legh, his wife, and their daughters Alice and Beata, were all brilliant archers, occupying much the same position in the archery world as the Dods

Annie (head up for the photographer) at the billiards table.

had once occupied in the tennis world, in as much as their presence at any tournament was enough to raise the level of excitement. Indeed, the elder daughter, Alice Blanche, was one of the finest archers that this country has produced in the recorded history of the sport, winning the Grand National Archery Society Ladies' Championship of the United Kingdom on twenty-three occasions between 1881 and 1922.

Lottie and her brothers do not appear to have shot at any club ground before they moved to Newbury, but they joined the recently-formed Welford Park Archers as soon as they had settled into their new home.

Fairly unusual for the time in admitting both sexes as members, Welford Park Archers was a small archery society that met in idyllic surroundings in Welford Park, near Newbury.

In 1906 Lottie announced her arrival on the national archery scene by emerging from an entry of ninety-nine competitors as the winner of The Royal Toxophilite Society Ladies' Day Gold Medal.

In 1906, 1907 and 1908 she won Fifth place in the Grand National Archery Meeting. With entries in the eighties and nineties, her performances were nothing if not respectable.

Perhaps a note on archery tournaments and the scoring system should be included here for the benefit of those who are unfamiliar with the sport.

Annie aged about forty.

1906. Welford Park Archers. Lottie extreme left, front row. Willie extreme right, front row. Tony standing back to tree.

Until 1908 shooting outside the ninety or so private archery societies that existed in Edwardian times was limited to The National Championship, four regional championships, and a few special meetings, such as the Hereford Round Meeting and The Royal Toxophilite Society's Ladies' Day Meeting.

Most of these public meetings allocated two days for the Championships, shooting a single round each day. Gentlemen shot the York Round of 144 arrows in the order of six dozen at 100 yards; four dozen at 80 yards, and two dozen at 60; Ladies shot the National Round of four dozen at 60 yards, and two dozen at 50. The Hereford Round Meeting for ladies gave them the opportunity to shoot at longer distances than 60 yards by starting with six dozen at 80 yards, followed by four dozen at 60, and two dozen at 50 yards.

Targets were — and are — marked outwards from the gold at the centre in bands of red, blue, black and white. Nine points are awarded for hitting the gold; seven for red; five for blue; three for black and one for white.

The only significant difference between tournaments in the Dods' time and modern tournaments is to be found in the old practice of shooting "ends" of three arrows alternately at targets placed at each end of the shooting ground, which was abandoned in favour of one-way shooting in 1949.

The winners were not always those making the top scores. Instead, there was a system of points awarded for the best score at each distance, most hits, and so on, and a percentage deductions handicapping system.

Archery was the one major sport in which Lottie was overshadowed by another member of the Family. During the four year period when he shot in open competitions, Willy was to prove himself the most formidable bowman in the Kingdom. Using self yew bows of 50lbs to 55lbs draw-weight pull and 4/9d arrows (i.e. weighing the equivalent of four old shilling and ninepence in silver coins, say two florins, a six-penny piece, and a silver threepenny bit), except at 60 yards, when he used 5/3d long-fletched ones, he finished every tournament he entered either as winner or runner-up. Shooting in a club competition at Welford Park, he once recorded two dozen at 60 yards, totalling 182, the first dozen being 98, a score that represents a very impressive achievement with wooden gear.

Tony, too, was a top archer. Examination of Welford Park records show that he edged Willy into second place in more than one club tournament. If his record in public meetings is rather less impressive than that of Willy or Lottie, it is, at least partly, due to the fact that he entered fewer. Suffering from a heart problem, he found the sheer physical effort of drawing a bow over two days exhausting.

In 1908 Willy and Lottie entered the first Ranelagh Club Open Meeting, held on the 2nd and 3rd June.

Designed to increase the number of occasions when archers from the various clubs could meet to compete against each other, the first Ranelagh Open Meeting attracted 123 entries from Ladies, and 30 from gentlemen, including the reigning men's National Champion, H.P. Nesham, several past National Champions, and most of the leading archers of the day. Men were required to shoot the Double York Round, and ladies to shoot the Double National.

After two days of competition in fine weather, Willy emerged as the winner of the men's rounds by the convincing margin of fifty-five points over the runner-up, but again Lottie secured the now-familiar Fifth Place from the much bigger field in the ladies' rounds.

In passing, it is sad to note that the Ranelagh Meeting did not become established as a permanent feature of the Archery Calendar. Although the four meetings which followed were well supported, for reasons that do not seem to have been recorded, no meetings were held in 1913 or 1914, or in the years immediately following The First World War. In 1929 the Event was revived and held annually until 1933, after which it was again discontinued. The last attempt to restore the Ranelagh Meeting to the Archery Calendar was made in 1947, but only one tournament was held.

Lottie and Willy both shot so well in the early part of the season that they were selected to represent the United Kingdom in the archery events at the 1908 Olympic Games.

Staged in London, the Games were centred on a new purpose-built stadium at Shepherd's Bush — later to become familiar as The White City Stadium — with the archery tournament held on July 17th and 18th. It was the fourth modern Olympiad, and the first to include events for women competitors.

Although the Games as a whole attracted more countries and more competitors than any of the previous Games, entries for the Archery Competitions were disappointing. With national teams limited to thirty competitors, fifteen archers shot for Britain in the men's event, eleven for France, and one from the United States, while the twenty-five British women competitors were left to shoot against each other. Not only that, for some reason or other, none of the Legh Family was present.

The weather, too, was disappointing. So cold and wet were the Archery Competition days that the stands were all but deserted.

On the Friday frequent rain squalls swept the stadium, stopping the shooting and making the competitors run for cover, and when it was not actually raining, the wind continued to gust and eddy in the bowl of the arena, producing extremely difficult conditions for shooting.

Even so, the competitors presented a brave show in the midst of the desolation as, dressed in their bright Edwardian finery, they

1908. Lottie shooting at the Olympic games.

struggled gallantly on to complete their alloted tasks: the men to shoot the York Round; the ladies to shoot the National.

From the Dods' point of view the day ended very satisfactorily with both Willy and Lottie leading the fields in their respective competitions.

The first day's totals were:

Gentlemen	Hits	Score
W. Dod (Welford Park Archers)	91	403
R. Brooks-King (West Somerset Archers)	93	393
J. Penrose (Wiltshire Archery Society)	90	364
Ladies		
Miss L. Dod (Welford Park Archers)	66	348
Miss Q. Newall (Cheltenham Archers)	66	338
Mrs. Wadworth (Hereford Bowmen)	66	310

"Inherited Archery" read the caption above *The Times* report. It continued, "Both contests were very pretty and graceful exhibitions and some exceptionally good shooting was seen. The first place in each was taken by a member of the same family, Mr. W. Dod and Miss L. Dod, a result doubtless traceable to the law of inherited tendency."

Possibly the journalist concerned wrote truer than he knew; possibly the shade of Sir Antony Dod stood smiling behind his descendants as they added further lustre to the Family name.

If so, his smile must have faded somewhat on the Saturday. In weather conditions that were only marginally better than those of the previous day, Lottie failed to maintain her lead and was overtaken by Queenie Newall, who finished the day forty-three points ahead of her.

Once again the Press rushed to commiserate with Lottie.

"While congratulating Miss Newall, whose rise to prominence in the archery world has been of unprecedented quickness", remarked *The Ladies' Field*, "It is impossible to withold one's sympathy for Miss Dod, who has come so tantalisingly near to crowning her many athletic feats with a win in what may truthfully be called the archery championship of the World." (1st August, 1908).

If there was in the sentiments the underlying suggestion that Queenie Newall's triumph was likely to prove an isolated achievement, the writer was mistaken. In the years that followed she showed herself to be a very fine archer indeed, winning the Grand National Archery Championship twice, and outshooting the great Alice Blanche Legh on a number of occasions. There was no disgrace for Lottie in losing to Miss Newall.

In the meantime, Willy had pressed on to win his event by a very comfortable margin. In beating Richard Brooks-King into second place, he defeated a four times Champion of the Grand National Archery Society, and an archer was who was destined to win it on five more occasions. The Bronze Medal was won by the current United States Champion, H.B. Richardson.

The final totals were:

Gentlemen	Hits	Scores	Golds
W. Dod (Welford Park Archers)	185	815	13
R. Brooks-King (West Somerset Archers)	184	768	7
H.B. Richardson (United States)	170	760	8
Ladies			
Miss Q. Newall (Cheltenham Archers)	132	688	23
Miss L. Dod (Welford Park Archers)	126	642	16
Miss Hill-Lowe (Archers of the Teme)	118	618	15

Disappointing as it must have been for Lottie, she and Willy did manage to establish a rather curious sort of record. Nearly eighty years later, the following paragraph appeared in *The Daily Telegraph* during the Los Angeles Olympiad of 1984. "Family Double Sets a Puzzle. Al Joyner and his sister, Jackie, completed a family double that had Olympic record-keepers scratching their heads. Al took the gold in the triple jump and Jackie the silver in the heptathlon to become the first brother and sister pairing to win Olympic honours on the same day, Saturday.

Officials in Los Angeles searched the history books but could find no other instance of such a family feat." (5th August, 1984).

Obviously, they did not search thoroughly.

Incidently, the 1908 Olympics was the first at which medals were awarded.

There may have been some slight consolation for Lottie in the fact that earlier in the season she had won the 1908 Southern Counties Ladies' Championship, while the best that Willy had been able to manage in the Gentlemen's rounds had been runner-up.

In 1909 Willy shot at the Grand National Archery Meeting for the first time, and, after an exciting contest he wrested the title from the reigning Champion, Richard Brooks-King, his former Olympic opponent.

Lottie had to be satisfied with sixth place in the Ladies' rounds. The Grand National Archery Meeting was the only tournament at which she shot that year.

She may well have decided that her relatively low placing in the 1909 National Championship was partly due to lack of major tournament practice because in the earlier part of the following season she entered three of the five regional meetings, and the Hereford meeting, by way of preparation for the big event. She was runner-up at the Hereford Meeting; gained Third Place at the Southern Counties Meeting; and was placed sixth at both the Leamington and Midland Counties Meeting and the Northern Counties Meeting. The final results of these tournaments are, however, somewhat misleading. Close examination of the scores published in *The Archer's Register* show that on all those occasions she had experienced difficulty in maintaining her efforts over the two days competition of major tournaments. In almost every case, at the end of the first day's shooting she had been one of the two leading archers, but she had fallen back during the second day's shooting, just as she had done at the Olympic Games.

Willy won the Southern Counties Archery Championship at the only regional meeting where he shot during the year.

When the 1910 Grand National Archery Meeting opened on Clifton College Cricket Ground on 10th August, 1910, their respective forms were such that Willy was generally favoured to retain the Men's Championship, but Lottie — if she were considered at all — was probably regarded as having no more than an outside chance of winning the Ladies' Championship. Few could have

THE HEREFORD ROUND MEETING.

1910 The Hereford Round Meeting at Shrewsbury. Lottie (seated left) chats to some of the other competitors.

guessed that they might achieve the sort of triumph that had eluded them at the Olympic Games.

Yet such appeared to be the case at the end of the first day's shooting. With fields of ninety-six ladies and fifty gentlemen, Lottie had built up a lead of twenty-six points over the second-placed lady, Mrs. Wadsworth, and Willy was leading his old rival, Brooks-King, by thirteen points.

The totals at the end of the first day (first six places) were:

Gentlemen	Hits	Score
W. Dod	99	449
R. Brooks-King	92	436
J.B. Keyworth	88	414
W. Inderwick	81	377
R.O. Backhouse	81	371
Parker Evans	79	355

Ladies	Hits	Score
Miss Dod	68	406
Mrs. Wadsworth	70	380
Mrs. C. Bowly	69	377
Mrs. G. Honeywill	69	369
Miss Q. Newall	66	362
Miss Legh	71	349

Lottie and Willy walked to the targets for the second day's shooting knowing they had the opportunity to create an archery legend.

It was not to be. While Willy continued to flight his duel with Brooks-King, Lottie struggled to overcome her old problem, but both finished their rounds as runners-up.

The scores for the end of the second day (first six places) were:

Gentlemen	Hits	Score
R. Brooks-King	101	453
W. Dod	103	433
W. Inderwick	95	425
J.B. Keyworth	86	422
Elton Lee	90	398
H.P. Nesham	84	362

Ladies	Hits	Score
Mrs. Wadsworth	69	373
Miss Legh	68	354
Mrs. R. Sandford	66	348
Mrs. G. Honnywill	63	339
Miss Dod	66	336
Miss Q. Newall	59	331

With the scores totalled and adjusted the final results (first three places) were:

Gentlemen	Hits	Score	Golds
R. Brooks-King	193	889	14
W. Dod	202	882	12
J.B. Keyworth	174	836	16
Ladies			
Mrs. Wadsworth	139	753	20
Miss Dod	134	742	20
Mrs. G. Honnywill	132	708	13

Just how close Lottie and Willy came to achieving the double may be judged by comparing the scores of winner and runner-up in each round, and then comparing them with the margin which separated the runner-up from the third-placed archer in each case.

In archery terms 1911 was a year of very mixed fortunes for the Dods. Lottie shot at four of the regional meetings, but without distinction. Consistent as ever, Willy retained the Southern Counties Archery Championship, and regained the Grand National Archery Championship. For the first time, Tony entered the Grand National Meeting and finished in Fifth Place, as he did in the two following years.

1911 also marked the point at which the Dods' collective interest in top competition archery began to wane. Willy's appearance at the

Grand National Meeting, 1911. Willy on left nearest camera.

1911 Grand National Meeting was his last in an open tournament; Lottie's last appearance was at the 1912 Grand National Meeting, where she was unplaced; and Tony made his final appearance at the 1913 Grand National Archery Meeting.

Although there may have been several reasons for this, fairly sudden, loss of interest in archery, the principal one appears to have been the dissolution of Welford Park Archers at the end of 1911. For Lottie and her brothers the Club had been the foundation on which all their archery activities — and much more — had been based. Lively and friendly, with a full programme of both archery and social events, Welford Park Archers appears to have catered for the needs of its members as few archery societies of the time seem to have done. Dances, picnics, novelty cricket matches between teams of lady and gentlemen members and occasional chess/bridge evenings in the winter, added a dimension to club life that appealed to many.

It is possible that more than one marriage originated in friendships which began at Welford Park, but one certainly did. It was as fellow members of the Club that Tony and his future wife met. Evelyn Frances Howard, the third daughter of the Reverend Henry Howard, Rector of nearby Brightwalton, was not only a keen archer but a very capable musician, playing the church organ and piano with equal facility. In addition to archery, she and Tony shared an interest in church work and, no doubt, their courtship blossomed as they busied

Brightwalton, 1908. Welford Park Archery Society. Annual Ladies v Gentlemen Cricket Match played in Rectory grounds at the invitation of Rev. Henry Howard.

themselves around and about the Reverend Howard's Parish as well as on the shooting ground. Incidentally, Evelyn was to die in 1986 at the age of 102.

It is also possible that it was during those Newbury days that Lottie gave some thought to the possibilities of matrimony. Many years later she told Tony's daughter-in-law, Joy — Michael Dod's wife — that she had turned down a proposal from a guards officer because he was the same age as she was, and she believed that a husband should always be older than his wife. Just who the soldier was is no longer known, but two of the Howard sons were in the Army, and it may well have been one of their colleagues who was interested in Lottie.

Almost certainly, Walford Park Archers ceased to exist because the Club had failed to secure a renewal of its lease. Unlike some archery societies, it did not own its shooting ground, but rented it from the owner of Welford Park, and he seems to have decided that he needed the area concerned for some other purpose.

That the Club was under notice to quit is suggested by the fact that towards the end of the 1911 season, some members applied for membership of other clubs. Among them was Willy, who was nominated for membership of the all-male Royal Toxophilite Society by his brother-in-law, Ernest Worssam, and elected a member on 11th August, 1911. Others, including Lottie, attempted to found a new club at Highclere, some ten miles from Welford, but without success. Possibly because they knew that they would be moving to Nether Stowey, in Somerset, after their wedding, Tony and Evelyn did not trouble to look for another club in the Berkshire area.

It seems, however, that for the Dods there could be no substitute for Welford Park. They were thoroughly disheartened by its disappearance, and their shooting during 1912 showed it.

Willy turned up at the Royal Toxophilite Society's ground on a few occasions, but he entered no open meetings and forfeited his Grand National Championship by default.

Tony won fifth place at the Grand National Archery Meetings of 1912 and 1913, but they were the only open Tournaments he entered during those seasons, and the final two open events at which he shot.

Lottie shot at three meetings in 1912, but with a marked lack of success. After having secured a place in the first half dozen national averages in every previous year when she had shot at open meetings, she could only manage thirty-fourth place in 1912.

That Willy should have laid down his competition bow when he was at the height of his powers might seem much more surprising than Lottie abandoning archery when she had lost the ability to shoot high scores. After all, he had good reason to believe that he could continue to win the Grand National Archery Championship for many more years.

Willy Dod.

But that was not how the Dods looked at sport. When they no longer enjoyed playing at a particular sport they stopped playing it, irrespective of whether they were in good or poor form at the time. Lottie abandoned competition tennis and hockey when she was playing supremely well; she stopped playing golf and archery after a series of setbacks. Winning or losing, it was whether they enjoyed the game or not that mattered. Of course, they were competitive and they liked to win, but the important challenge — the element that yielded most pleasure — was the challenge of proving something to themselves. Pot hunting they regarded with contempt. Had Willy been so inclined he could, presumably, have toured the open competitions collecting championships, but once he had established himself among the country's leading archers he confined his entries to his own — Southern Counties-Archery Meeting, and the Grand National Archery Meeting.

Even so, Lottie's failure to win a major archery championship must have been a considerable disappointment for her. The more so because her retirement from all competition sport, and her long and distinguished career, which came so close to ending in the glory of yet another national championship or an Olympic title, petered out in the obscurity which is born of lost ability.

But, in the last analysis, Lottie's failure to win a major archery championship is not enough to undermine her stature as an athlete. It is based, too firmly for that, on her incredible versatility. Having proved herself without equal in her own discipline of tennis, she proceeded to play with and against the top players in other sports on equal terms. Lady Margaret Scott, May Hezlet, Alice Blanche Legh, and many others who are still regarded as great sportswomen, found in her a worthy opponent. There was, however, one important difference between Lottie Dod and her distinguished contemporaries: they were great golfers, archers, hockey players, and so on, but she was a great athlete.

Chapter Eight

This final chapter is by way of being an epilogue. Although Lottie's days on the national sports scene lay behind her by 1914, it seems fitting to conclude this "Story of an Athlete" with a summary of her later years, which were far from lacking incident or interest.

A year or so after Tony and Evelyn had set up home at Nether Stowey, Lottie and Willy also moved westwards to Bideford, drawn, at least partly, by the lush fairways of The Royal North Devon Golf Club at Westward Ho!, a course which they both loved. They bought a house at nearby Bideford, overlooking the River Torridge, and in 1913 they reinforced the high standing which their reputations had obliged local golfers to accord them on their arrival by winning the championships of the Men's and Ladies' clubs respectively. They also played a considerable amount of social tennis and croquet, and Lottie bought a horse to ride in the surrounding countryside.

For all that, they were not so besotted with sport that they were unaware of world events. That would have been almost impossible. By 1913 it had become clear that war in Europe was inevitable and the nation had begun to brace itself for the conflict.

Lottie prepared to play her part when war came by attending first-aid and home nursing classes, and she gained a St. John's Ambulance certificate in these subjects.

Despite this training, however, it was several months after the outbreak of hostilities in August 1914 before she was able to find employment with any of the nursing services.

This was in marked contrast to Willy's experience. Although he was then aged 47, Willy was able to enlist without difficulty as a private in the 23rd (Service) 1st Sportsman's Battalion, The Royal Fusiliers, just four weeks after war was declared, and before the end of the year he was in France.

During August 1914 Lottie stayed with Tony and Evelyn for a fortnight and met their second child Philip, who had been born in July.

"Was introduced to Philip William," she wrote in the Visitors' Book on the 24th August. "Fell violently in love (for the first time). They say with truth that 'a mother's love is nearest to the love that angels bear' — at the same time they might add something nice about an auntie's feelings."

Started immediately after Tony and Evelyn set up home and maintained throughout their married lives, this Visitors' Book contains a number of interesting entries made by Lottie and Willy.

It reveals, for example, that either Lottie found baby Philip irresistible or she missed Willy's companionship after he had

1914 Private William Dod.

enlisted, or both. Whatever the reason, she spent a considerable amount of time at Tony's in the second half of the year. An entry in the Guest Book made at the end of a visit which lasted from September 17th to the 29th, 1914, reads:

"The third visit within ten weeks. Hope they are not fair sick of me."

In December she was accepted by the Red Cross Society to work as a non-uniformed volunteer in a temporary military hospital at Speen, near her old home at Newbury.

As for Willy, it seems that a few weeks in the trenches had been enough to convince him, as it had convinced many another soldier, that he should have joined the Navy. Somewhat surprisingly, his application for a transfer was successful. He must have learned of his transfer while he was on leave from France and staying with Tony and Evelyn from 22nd to 30th April, 1915, because his entry in the Visitors' Book reads,

"Arrived a 'Tommy'. Left a sailor."

He was, in fact, commissioned in the R.N.V.R. and posted back to France later in the year to do administrative work with the Royal Naval Air Service.

In 1916 he was invalided out of the Navy for reasons that are no longer known, illegally taking his rifle with him.

Meanwhile, Lottie performed the miscellaneous tasks that were assigned to her at Speen, with growing impatience while she tried to secure a transfer to a hospital in France. Her prospects can hardly have been helped by a bout of sciatica which prostrated her in July, 1915. After being confined to her bed for several weeks she travelled to Nether Stowey to convalesce.

"Arrived looking rather decayed after long sciatica illness," she wrote at the end of her month's stay. "Left in rude health: the result of pints (or was it quarts) of clotted cream, of delicious delicacies, and lovely walks in the grand Quantock Country."

She also added, with obvious irritation, that she was returning to Speen and not going to "the Front".

Her first application for a transfer was refused — almost certainly because of her 43 years and her susceptibility to sciatica attacks — but she renewed her requests and, despite repeated refusals by the Red Cross, continued to do so.

In November, 1916 she attempted to improve her chances of being sent to France by enrolling as a uniformed volunteer, but she was disappointed. Instead of being sent to France, she was posted to Number 72 Voluntary Aid Detachment Hospital at Chelsea as a

1916 Lottie in Red Cross uniform.

pantrymaid/housemaid. In this her situation was in marked contrast to that of her old tennis opponent Maude Watson, who, with no better training, commanded the Berkswell Auxiliary Hospital. Of course, the fact that Maude owned the building in which the Hospital was housed might have had something to do with her appointment.

In the event, Lottie was destined never to see wartime France. Another sciatica attack in April, 1918, was so severe that she was persuaded to resign from the Red Cross.

On that occasion she spent her period of convalescence with the recently-widowed Annie and her family at "Pyrcroft", the fine Tudor house at Chertsey, where the Worssams had lived since Ernest's retirement in 1912. Her stay of three or four months gave small pleasure to Annie's teenage sons, Ray and Geoffrey, who were required to surrender their own, very comfortable bedroom, to their aunt, and move into the spare room.

Fully recovered, Lottie joined Willy at Bideford in October.

For her contribution to the war effort Lottie was presented with. the British Red Cross Society's Service Medal 1914-18, which was awarded to volunteers who had completed a thousand hours, or more, war service.

After the Armistice Lottie decided to return to London, while Willy opted to remain in Devon. That being so, in August 1919, they sold their house at Bideford, and Willy bought a flat at Westward Ho! which he whimsically named "The Divot", while Lottie returned to the Capital.

On her way she stopped to spend a holiday with Tony and Evelyn, "Am an 'omeless orphan. Don't even own a doll's house now," she wailed in the Visitors' Book.

It was a problem that was soon solved. Back in London she bought a flat and turned again to two of her long-standing interests, tennis and singing.

Between the Wars she played a great deal of tennis at the Roehampton Club, where she was a member, and she attended every Wimbledon Tournament as a spectator until she was well into her eighties.

Together with the other surviving past Wimbledon Champions, Lottie was presented with a sterling silver commemorative medal on the Centre Court at the All England Club's new Church Road Ground by King George V and Queen Mary on the occasion of the Silver Jubilee Championships of 1926. There she met many of her old opponents — some of whom she had not seen for twenty years and more — including Maude Watson and Blanche Hillyard.

Another rather poignant meeting took place at the Roehampton Club in 1929 when, completely by chance, Lottie met Charlotte

Sterry (née Cooper) who, at the turn of the century, had also held the Wimbledon title five times. Asked by some of the members present to play an exhibition set, the former champions refused to play singles — they were, after all, both well on the wrong side of fifty — but, each taking a young woman member as a partner, they played a doubles. As customary on those sort of occasions, the result was not recorded.

For some years in the twenties and thirties Lottie was a member of two distinguished choirs, "The Oriana Madrigal Society" and "The Bach Cantata Club", which performed in many concert halls in and around London, and she sang with the Bach Club when it gave a recital before King George V and Queen Mary in the Chapel at Buckingham Palace on Wednesday 16th March 1927. Unfortunately, no record of the programme or the performance now exists. At some time or other Vaughan Williams heard Lottie sing solo, because a note among her papers mentions that the composer had liked her voice.

1929. At the Roehampton Club. Charlotte Sterry (second left). Five times Wimbledon Champion and Lottie Dod (extreme right). Five Times Wimbledon Champion and partners.

Although Lottie continued to visit Annie after the War, she spent rather more time with Tony and Evelyn because she enjoyed the company of their children: Barbara who had been born in 1913; Philip, born in 1914, Michael born in 1915; and Geoffrey, who was born in 1921. By that time, of course, the Worssam children were young adults.

In late 1919 Tony and Evelyn had moved from Somerset to Kilmeston, Hampshire.

Re-named "Edgeway" by Tony to conform with family tradition, their newly-acquired house was a substantial place, standing in twenty acres.

It was land enough for the Dods to keep a few cows, some poultry, and over forty beehives, and for Tony to employ a gardener/handyman and a boy.

It was also land enough to afford the Family plenty of room for recreational purposes. There was a grass tennis court, lawns that could be used for bowling and putting, and a "Long Meadow", which was ideal for archery practice. In addition, a badminton court was laid out in a barn that had been placed at their disposal by a friendly neighbour.

Unfortunately for the children, the "Edgeworth" Dods lacked the patience to be good instructors. Their own reactions naturally razor-sharp, they could not even begin to analyse the children's difficulties. On one occasion Lottie made a determined attempt to solve Michael Dod's tennis problems by playing him left-handed. He was then in his mid-teens — about the same age that Lottie had been when she was winning major tournaments — and she was in her mid-fifties, but she still won. The Worssam children's experience had been much the same. Ray Worssam recalls that on many occasions Annie — a formidable player — tried to teach him to play auction bridge with a complete lack of success. "You should play the Queen on that trick," she might say to him, but he could never understand how his mother knew he had the Queen. In 1925, when he was twenty-four and she was sixty-one, Annie ran him off the tennis court.

Not that most of the Dod/Worssam children would have made any better progress if gifted instructors had been available. Only Barbara Dod, who became a county standard archer, and Michael Dod, who was a very capable long distance cyclist, seem to have inherited any of the "Edgeworth" Dods' facility for sport.

In 1927 the Family suffered a great blow when, after a short illness, Annie died of cancer.

The outbreak of The Second World War found Lottie still living in London and, despite the Blitz, it was 1942 before Willy could persuade her to join him in Devon.

91

Annie.

Meanwhile, Willy himself had wiped the grease off his Lee-Enfield and joined the Home Guard. No doubt, if the worst had come to the worst, and he had exhausted his ammunition, he could have startled Hitler's legions with his long-bow.

After the War Lottie and Willy continued to live at Westward Ho! for some years. In 1948 Willy was elected President of The Royal North Devon Golf Club, and in the following year Lottie was elected President of The Royal North Devon Ladies' Golf Club.

In 1950, Lottie bought a flat in Earl's Court, London, and she divided her time between London and Devon, until 1952 when Willy gave up his flat and joined her in London.

In 1946, when the Wimbledon Tournament was resumed after the War, Lottie took her seat in the Members' Gallery and continued to do so almost to the end of her life.

In an article published in 1953, Arthur Herschell, Vice-President of The Lawn Tennis Association, and a friend of Lottie's from their Rock Ferry Tennis Club days, commented that Lottie had remained a very shrewd judge of the Game.

"A year or two ago I asked Miss Dod if she could compare some of the leading players of her day with those of today and she wisely pointed out that it was really impossible to make comparisons. How can one compare the periods of the horse, steam engine, electric motor, and aeroplane? She says the standard of women's play at lawn tennis has, of course, improved enormously since her day. Her best antagonists served overhead, but never hit hard, like present-day players. Neither did they employ the lob as well, nor really drive a back-hand stroke off the ground. In her day the players had very good forehand strokes and, in her opinion, judged the length of the court better than most of the present women players. Many of the women of her day volleyed quite well, but not severely enough." (*Cheshire Life February 1953*).

On 8th October, 1954 Willy died at the Earl's Court flat.

After his death Lottie moved from one south-coast nursing home to another, including one at Eastbourne where she was attended by Dr. John Bodkin Adams, who was later to become the central figure in a sensational murder trial, before she settled on Birchy Hill Nursing Home at Sway, where she was close to Tony and Evelyn. There, several journalists — including some very well known names associated with the B.B.C. — sought interviews with her, but these she steadfastly refused to give. Delighted, as she invariably was, to exchange courtesies with any caller and even to pose for photographs, the reluctance which she had always shown to talk about herself had hardened into a determination not to do so.

On 7th January, 1960, Tony died.

Tony.

Lottie herself died on the following 27th June, her passing saluted by the sounds of Wimbledon. She slipped quietly away while she was resting in bed and listening to the radio broadcast from the tournament. She was in her eighty-ninth year.

1937 Lottie and Willy and an unknown friend.

OTHER TITLES FROM
Countyvise

Local History

Birkenhead Priory	£1.80
The Spire is Rising	£1.95
The Search for Old Wirral	£9.95
Birkenhead Park	£1.40
A Guide to Merseyside's Industrial Past	£1.95
Neston and Parkgate	£2.00
Scotland Road	£5.95
Helen Forrester Walk	£1.00
Women At War	£2.95
Merseyside Moggies	£1.00
Dream Palaces	£7.50
Forgotten Shores	£3.25

Local Shipping Titles

Sail on the Mersey	£1.95
The Mersey at Work — Ferries	£1.40
Ghost Ships on the Mersey	£1.40
The Liners of Liverpool — *Part 1*	£2.95
The Liners of Liverpool — *Part II*	£2.95
The Liners of Liverpool — *Part III*	£2.95

Local Railway Titles

Seventeen Stations to Dingle	£2.95
The Line Beneath the Liners	£2.95
Steel Wheels to Deeside	£2.95
Seaport to Seaside	£4.25
Northern Rail Heritage	£1.95
A Portrait of Wirral's Railways	£3.95

History with Humour

The One-Eyed City	£2.95
Hard Knocks	£3.95
The Binmen are Coming	£3.50

Natural History

Birdwatching in Cheshire	£3.95

Other Titles

Speak through the Earthquake, Wind & Fire	£3.95
It's Me, O Lord	£0.40
Companion to the Fylde	£1.75
Country Walks on Merseyside	£1.95